STUDIES IN THE BRITISH ECONOMY

National income and expenditure in Britain and OECD countries

by
Samuel Hays

*Formerly Head of the Central Statistics Branch
Ministry of Supply and Ministry of Aviation,
Formerly Senior Research Officer, National
Institute of Economic and Social Research*

HEINEMANN EDUCATIONAL
BOOKS LTD · LONDON

Heinemann Educational Books Ltd
LONDON EDINBURGH MELBOURNE TORONTO
AUCKLAND SINGAPORE JOHANNESBURG
HONG KONG NAIROBI IBADAN NEW DELHI

ISBN 0 435 84544 6

Samuel Hays 1971
First published 1971

Published by Heinemann Educational Books Ltd
48 Charles Street, London W1X 8AH
Printed in Great Britain by Cox and Wyman Ltd
London, Fakenham and Reading

NATIONAL INCOME AND EXPENDITURE IN BRITAIN AND OECD COUNTRIES

STUDIES IN THE BRITISH ECONOMY
General Editor: *Derek Lee*

CONTENTS

PREFACE

Most economics text books attempt to cover the subject within a single volume and in consequence some topics are treated briefly: often these same topics are those whose subject matter changes most rapidly. At present in order to keep up to date in the field of economics recourse must be made to a vast field of diffused literature including bank reviews, government publications, newspapers and various journals. With these problems in mind this series was conceived. The series consists of specialized books on those topics which are subject to frequent change or where the sources of information are too scattered to be readily available to the average student. It is intended that each book will be revised at frequent intervals in order to take account of new developments.

The books are written with the needs of Advanced Level candidates especially in mind, but they also cover the ground for many professional examinations in economics and first-year university students will also find them valuable.

Derek Lee
General Editor

AUTHOR'S NOTE

The subject matter of this little book is of comparatively recent origin and its publication represents the first systematic presentation of the study for young economists who are still at school, or studying for the professions. It is essentially an analysis of a large mass of related statistics – but an analysis directed towards the isolation and verification of a few fundamental economic principles. Moreover, many of the figures put forward and discussed are of great intrinsic interest and value: they form an essential part of one's understanding of the economic life of the country as it is today.

The author would like to acknowledge the permission given by HMSO for the reproduction of much copyright material.

Samuel Hays

Part 1 The Theory and Background of National Income Accounts

CHAPTER 1
THE PLACE AND IMPORTANCE OF NATIONAL INCOME STUDIES

Introduction

Since the end of the Second World War there has been an enormous development in the study of econometrics, or numerical economics. 'This is a branch of economics in which economic theory, mathematics, and statistics are fused in the analysis of numerical and institutional data. Econometrics presents economic theories in a form in which they can be tested statistically against observed events.'[1] National income accounting or measurement is, perhaps, the most important branch of econometrics. The rapid expansion of such measurement has made it possible to focus interest on economic growth, and to identify the industrial and functional sources of this growth. Economic growth has come to be assessed by growth in the gross national product – or the monetary value set on all the goods and services produced in the country in a given period, usually a year. The economic well-being of the inhabitants of Britain and of all countries has come to be identified, and even measured, by the gross national product per head; or rather, the expenditure on consumer goods and services per head of the population.

At the same time, the prevalent ideas concerning the means of increasing gross national product and of sharing it more fairly have become more and more precise. The view is now widely held that the better any country is able to measure changes in its national output and to identify the share of such changes attributable to such factors as, for example, consumers' expenditure, investment, public expenditure, and exports, then the better that country will be able to stimulate this growth. In addition, wealth and welfare comparisons between countries have been made possible by national income studies. The world-wide interest in this branch of economics is shown by the fact that no

---

[1] *Dictionary of Economics*, Seldon and Pennance, J. M. Dent

fewer than 100 countries or states now provide estimates of their gross national product at current and constant prices to the United Nations Secretariat, and these are published in the Monthly Statistical Bulletins and the Yearbooks of the United Nations.

No student of economics can claim, nowadays, to have even an elementary working knowledge of his subject unless he has some acquaintance with this branch of econometrics. Not only are national income studies valuable for their own sake, but they enable many economic theories to be put to the test of practical measurement. Such problems as the effect of investment on output, the kind of investment which is most conducive to economic growth, the changes which take place in the pattern of consumers' expenditure as a country achieves relative affluence, or the effect on national output of a large extension of centralized ownership and control, can find at least partial answers in national income studies. Perhaps most important of all, national income economics as we now know the subject owes its derivation to Keynesian discoveries and theories. At the same time, the successful operation of a growth policy based on such economics is the best possible indicator of their validity.

The importance of the national product or income in determining economic welfare was recognized long before the tools for measuring it had been forged. In *The Economics of Welfare* by Professor A. C. Pigou, first published in 1920, the author makes the point that 'generally speaking, economic causes act upon the welfare of any country, not directly, but through the making and using of that objective counterpart of economic welfare which economists call the national dividend or national income'. The whole framework around which *The Economics of Welfare* was written is that the economist must discover methods which will advance, and counsel the rejection of proposals which will hinder these three objects, namely: growth in the national income, the regularization of its flow through time, and the equalization of its distribution between persons.

Nearly two decades later, in 1937 Colin Clark first published his book, *National Income and Outlay*. In the introductory chapter of this book, Mr Clark refers to the earlier work by Professor Pigou, and in particular to the points emphasized in the preceding paragraph. To these he adds his own comment in these words: 'The propositions of economic science are largely concerned with questions of whether particular economic measures will have a beneficial or adverse effect upon the national income. The measurement of the national income (dividend) has hitherto been regarded as one of the

2

most difficult and uncertain branches of statistical science. As a result, economic theories are rarely put to the test of fact, and modern economics has shown a lop-sided development in an over-theoretical direction, of which outside critics justly complain.'

Mr Clark was one of the earlier pioneers who made national income accounting into a more exact science and his estimates of national income and expenditure in the twenties and early thirties are justly held in great respect. A decade before the publication of *National Income and Outlay*, two other famous economic statisticians, who in later years were given peerages for their services to the nation – the late Lords Stamp and Bowley – had estimated national income and outlay in the early twenties. But it was the general acceptance of Keynesian doctrines which really stimulated the study of national income accounting and put it in the forefront of aids to economic policy. In 1941 the Chancellor of the Exchequer, Sir Kingsley Wood, produced the first of the annual series of White Papers and Blue Books on the national income and expenditure. By this time, some of the country's most eminent economists and statisticians had been pressed into Government service.

After the war had ended and the United Nations Organization, with its agencies, had been set up, one of its earliest tasks was to set up a statistical advisory and executive service. Much time was spent in unifying definitions and methodology and in their dissemination throughout the world, with the result referred to in the second paragraph of this chapter. At home the Central Statistical Office was enlarged and undertook the work of compiling the national income accounts. Shortly after the end of the war, the annual White Papers became Blue Books, with the summary and preliminary estimates only appearing in White Papers. The scope and contents of the Blue Books have increased each year and the estimates have advanced a great deal in precision and accuracy.

Within recent years, economic researchers and statisticians have estimated the gross national product of the United Kingdom and of its main constituents right back to 1688, the year in which James II was forced into exile and William and Mary became joint rulers. The main source of such information is *British Economic Growth 1688–1959* (2nd edition), by P. M. Deane and W. A. Cole, and Appendix I quotes a number of salient facts from this most learned and valuable publication. *National Income and Expenditure of the United Kingdom 1870–1952*, by James B. Jefferys and Dorothy Walters (Reprint Series No. 6), is an excellent pamphlet published by NIESR.

3

Comparisons of output per head in Britain and ten other OECD countries over varying periods in the past century appeared in *Economic Review No. 16*, published by NIESR in July 1961. Extracts from this appear in Appendix II.

Macro-economics

The study of national income and expenditure provides the best example of macro-economics in practice. Macro-economics is not an easy concept for the student to understand; nevertheless, a definition may add something to the reader's appreciation of its significance. It may be defined as the study of human activities in large groups as indicated by economic aggregates such as total employment, national income, investment, consumption, prices, wages or costs. The purpose of macro-economic theory is to study systematically the influences which determine the levels of national income and other aggregates and the level of employment of resources. When these principles have been determined they may be, and are, used for economic forecasting and for the management of the economy. Macro-economics has its own rules because aggregate economic behaviour does not necessarily correspond to the total of individual activities. Thus, a fall in wages and production costs may lead to an increase in profitability, and therefore of employment, at a single firm, but total employment need not be increased by a fall in wages. The more traditional approach to economics is through the study of micro-economics, which concerns itself with the economic actions of individuals and of small groups.

CHAPTER 2
DEFINITIONS AND RELATIONSHIPS
IN NATIONAL INCOME
ACCOUNTING

The national income

The national income is a measure of the money value of goods and services becoming available to the nation from economic activity. But it is not simply an aggregate of all incomes. It includes only those incomes, whether individual or corporate, which are derived directly from the current production of goods and services. Such incomes are defined as factor incomes. Other forms of income, for example retirement pensions, family allowances, or receipts of private gifts, cannot be regarded as payments for current services to production. Such incomes are derived from taxation, National Insurance contributions, or the work and efforts of others, and as such are transfer incomes. The services of people who do not work for money, housewives for example, do not form part of the national income as these are not paid for. On the other hand, the wages paid to domestic servants are part of the national income.

One important form of income – interest and dividends – is capable of alternative treatments. Interest and dividends are paid out of profits which are factor incomes earned by the business employing the capital and making the profits. One could regard interest and dividends paid to individuals as unearned incomes of these individuals. All profits are not paid out as interest or dividends, and the undistributed profits can be regarded as the income of the firm or a form of corporate income. However, in Britain the whole of the profits made, whether distributed or not, are regarded as factor incomes of firms and enterprises, and interest and dividends received as transfer payments.

Some incomes which form part of the national income are imputed, rather than actual. Thus, a person who lives in a dwelling house or flat owned by him is regarded as receiving an income; if he were to let the house to another, he would receive rent: the imputed rent is the income he could expect to receive from such a letting.

The national income can be regarded in three ways. First, as a sum of incomes derived from economic activity. Such incomes can be broadly divided, for example between incomes from employment and incomes from profits. Second, the national income can be regarded as a sum of expenditure, for incomes must equal expenditure. Such expenditure can be divided into expenditure on consumption, or on the personal satisfaction of immediate wants, and expenditure on adding to wealth or investment. That part of incomes which is not spent on consumption or in buying capital equipment (investment) is sometimes called saving. Saving however, adds to wealth and to that extent is regarded as expenditure on adding to wealth. Third, the national income may be regarded as a sum of the products of the various manufacturing industries of the country and of the value of the services performed by the service industries and trades such as hairdressing, laundries, transport services, etc. (A moment's thought will show that the production of these goods and services provides the incomes received by individuals and firms.) But just as the national income is not simply an aggregation of all incomes, so the national income when regarded as an aggregation of output is not the sum total of the output of all industries. Such a total would include much double, treble, or even quadruple counting. Steel is manufactured and forms part of the output of the steel industry. Some of the steel so made goes into the production of ball-bearings which later are incorporated into the production of machinery. This double or treble counting is avoided if the aggregation is of the value added at each stage of manufacture.

Gross national product
At this point in our consideration of the national income a new concept must be introduced – gross national product. This is made up of gross domestic product together with net property income from abroad. If we consider the third method of arriving at the national income – the addition of the output, net of duplication, of all industries and sources, we arrive not at the true national income, but at the gross domestic product. A proportion of the output of goods and services is not regarded as being available for incomes, either personal or corporate. This proportion is used for the purpose of maintaining the nation's capital at its existing level. Capital equipment – buildings, plant and machinery, tools and equipment – is one of the factors of production, it assists in the production of wealth, and therefore is instrumental in providing incomes; but capital equipment wears out in use – buildings quite slowly, plant and machinery more quickly. It may also become out of date as new and improved machinery is in-

vented. The extent of this wear and obsolescence is called capital consumption. Gross domestic product minus capital consumption equals domestic income: domestic income plus income from abroad equals national income. National income is therefore that part of gross national product which is available for distribution as incomes, either personal or corporate. Nowadays gross domestic product and gross national product are regarded as more important and useful concepts than national income. Students familiar with accountancy terms and methods will recognize that capital consumption is equivalent to depreciation. Sums set aside for depreciation are set aside to maintain capital at its existing level.

Statistics of gross national product, national income and their constituents

Later chapters will deal in some detail with these constituents. At this point it will be useful to have some idea of their size. In 1968 the gross national product at factor cost was estimated to have amounted to £36,700 million, all but £420 million of which came from home sources; i.e. gross domestic product was £36,280 million. Capital consumption was estimated at £3,375 million, or about one-eleventh of gross national product. National income, or gross national product minus capital consumption, was therefore £33,325 million. In the earlier paragraphs of this chapter we have seen that gross national product can be regarded in three ways, the first being the sum of incomes derived from economic activity. Briefly, in 1968 income from employment was about £25,250 million, income from self-employment (private traders, partnerships, professional men) £2,840 million, gross trading profits of companies £5,120 million, gross trading profits of public corporations and enterprises £1,460 million, and income by way of rent, £2,360 million. These incomes total just over £37,000 million. Two adjustments have to be made, details of which will be made clear later, to arrive at a gross domestic product of £36,700 million.

The second way of looking at gross national product is from the expenditure and type of expenditure point of view. The two main types are expenditure on consumption and expenditure on capital equipment or investment. In 1968, expenditure by consumers (individuals satisfying their immediate wants) amounted to £22,200 million; expenditure by the Government and other public authorities such as local government bodies on current, i.e. non-investment, expenditure amounted to nearly £7,260 million, and £7,450 million was spent on capital investment by individuals, companies, public corporations (in the main the nationalized industries) and the Government and local authorities. These total nearly £37,000 million, but an adjustment has to be made in respect of expenditure on goods bought from abroad offset by receipts from goods sold abroad to reach a gross domestic product of £36,280 million.

The third way of arriving at gross domestic product is by adding together the net output or value added at each stage of manufacture. For this purpose, it is convenient to look at the value added by the main branches of economic activity: agriculture, mining and quarrying, manufacturing, building and construction, transport and communication, the buying and selling of goods, banking, insurance and other financial services, the services provided by the Government and local authorities such as defence, education, and health services and personal services such as laundries, hairdressers, etc. The most important contributor in the above list is manufacturing industry which, including the provision of gas, electricity and water, was about £13,825 million, or 38 per cent of gross domestic product. Buying and selling, or to use the more generalized term, distributive trades, accounted for £4,080 million, personal and other services for £4,730 million, and services provided by the Government and local authorities for £4,080 million. Agriculture, mining and quarrying provided only a modest contribution of £1,800 million, or only 5 per cent of gross domestic product, and out of this agriculture alone provided 3 per cent. Net income from abroad, of £420 million, provided about $1\frac{1}{4}$ per cent of gross national product.

Gross national product in relation to population

Gross national product per head of population, or national income per head, provide a measure of changing levels of output and living standards. In 1953 gross national product at factor cost was estimated at £15,075 million. By 1968, as we have already seen, it had risen to £36,700 million, an increase of 143 per cent. This rate of increase represents an annual average increase of nearly 6.25 per cent, quite a substantial amount.[1] But this increase is nominal rather than real; the quantity of goods and services produced in 1968 was not anywhere near 143 per cent greater than in 1953. The fact is that the same volume of goods and services cost 56 per cent more in 1968 than in 1953. This

---

[1] For the relevant formulae and methods of calculation see Appendix III.

process of price increases is known as inflation and more will be said about this at a later stage. If the effect of price increases is eliminated, the real increase in gross national product works out at 56 per cent, an average of 3·0 per cent a year. Over the fifteen year period, half the normal increase in gross national product was accounted for by price rises and half was a real increase. At the middle of 1953 the population of Britain was 50·7 million, fifteen years later it had grown to 55·3 million. Gross national product per head of population in 1953 was £300. In 1968 it was £665. When the effect of inflation is removed, the increase falls from 122 per cent to 42 per cent, or an average of 2·3 per cent a year. This is low compared with most industrial countries. In fact, Britain is either at the bottom, or near it, of the growth league table. (See Chapter 12 for the changes in gross national product per head for most countries of the Organization for European Co-operation and Development 1958–1968.)

Similar figures can be worked out for many other countries, but there are difficulties in comparing such figures with those worked out for Britain. The gross national product in each country is expressed in the currency of that country – dollars in the case of the United States, francs in France, marks in Germany, lire in Italy, and so on. These various currencies can be exchanged into British money, called sterling, at official rates of exchange. At the end of 1968, £1 was equivalent to 2·39 dollars, 11·80 francs, 9·52 marks, 1,487 lire; but this does not necessarily mean that 2·39 dollars buy the same volume of goods and services in the USA as £1 sterling does in Britain. More will be said about rates of exchange at a later stage in this book. Meanwhile, if we convert the gross national product per head expressed in these currencies to sterling at the current rate of exchange (this is the best we can do at the moment), the following ratios emerge:

Gross national product at factor cost per head in £'s sterling, 1968

United Kingdom	£ 665
USA	£1660
France	£ 895
Italy	£ 525
Japan	£ 550
Netherlands	£ 750
Sweden	£1185
Canada	£1160
Germany	£ 825

9

If the general level of prices in each of these countries were the same as in Britain, then production per head and income per head in USA was two and a half times, and in Canada, one and three quarters as great as in Britain (approx). There was little difference between production per head in France and Germany; both these countries are significantly more productive than Britain. Production per head in Italy and Japan was about four-fifths of that in Britain. It should be pointed out, though, that devaluation of sterling towards the end of 1967 adversely affected Britain's league position.

However, as we have seen, not all the gross national product is available for distribution as incomes. On the other hand, some wages and salaries may increase faster than gross national product per head. This must imply that others increase more slowly than gross national product per head, or that wages and salaries are taking a larger share of gross national product and profits a smaller share. Herein lies the source of some of the economic ills which have affected Britain for many years. But this will be further considered later on.

CHAPTER 3
STAGES IN ECONOMIC GROWTH

Introduction

In the first chapter we saw, in the words of Professor Pigou, that one object of economic policy should be to discover methods which will advance, and counsel the rejection of proposals which will hinder increases in the national income. Nowadays, the same idea is contained in the phrase 'fostering economic growth' to which a great deal of attention is paid. It is now generally recognized that the gross national product must be increased if individuals are to become better off, and present-day economic policy is directed towards this end. During the great depression which was experienced in the decade prior to the outbreak of the Second World War, it was often said that the root cause of the depression was over-production. Yet people in this and other industrial countries were not nearly so well off as now and production was not nearly so great. The connection between consumption, employment, income, and production was not then understood. More will be said about this connection later in this book. For the moment it should be pointed out that increased consumption, or the desire to increase consumption, can provide the urge towards greater production. Increased production is likely to lead to higher incomes and therefore to greater consumption, and so the motion of the economic cycle is continued and perhaps accelerated.

Wants and wealth

Economic growth is now considered to be economically, socially and even morally desirable. An increasing volume of material possessions is rightly considered as a means to a better life. This urge to enjoy greater wealth and prosperity is instinctive. Some economists express this idea by saying that 'wants' have no limit and that human activity is directed towards satisfying an ever-increasing proportion of these wants. There is a great disparity amongst the countries and races of mankind regarding the extent to which wants arise and are not satisfied. We saw in the last chapter that gross national product per head of population was about £665 in the United Kingdom in 1968; rather lower than other industrial countries in Western Europe and about

40 per cent of that in the United States. But compared with many countries in the world, the gross national product in Western Europe provides a very high standard of living. There are many countries in Africa and Asia with a gross national product per head in 1968 of one-tenth, or less, of that of Britain. This is true of the 1,300 million people in China, India, Pakistan and Indonesia, and of at least 250 million in Africa.

Under-developed and emergent countries

We can divide the main countries of the world into a small number of more or less homogeneous groups depending upon their economic development. Those countries with a gross national product of less than £100 per head are, in the main, agricultural countries operating a form of subsistence, or peasant farming. India, Pakistan, China and many African countries are examples of such countries. But the larger countries in this group are trying desperately to establish manufacturing industries of some kinds based on western practice. The poorer and smaller countries in this group have, as yet, not progressed beyond the stage of subsistence agriculture. Economic growth in this latter group can be initiated by the adoption of more efficient methods of farming and irrigation. However, tradition, ignorance, and poverty militate against such progress, and increases in gross national product are largely offset by increases in population; a situation not unlike that envisaged by the economist Malthus in Britain at the beginning of the 19th century.

Industrial take-off stage

The next stage in development is a more rapid industrial expansion once the industrial take-off point has been reached – i.e. sufficient capital equipment and industrial skills have been procured to permit some large-scale production in both primary and secondary industries. Agriculture is still very important, providing between 15 and 20 per cent of gross national product, and manufacturing industry between 25 and 30 per cent. Gross national product per head currently averages £250–£500 or so. Europe provides a number of examples – Spain, Austria, Finland and some Eastern Bloc countries. Outside Europe, Israel and South Africa would certainly qualify. Two countries, Italy and Japan, have recently graduated from this group to the next in order of industrialization – the advanced industrial countries. The economic experiences of these two countries (especially Japan) are very instructive.

Japan

In 1958, gross national product of factor cost per head in Japan was only £110, and recovery from war-time losses had not gone very far. Over the past decade, a relatively high proportion of the country's manpower has been efficiently mobilized for production and, as we have seen, gross national product per head exceeded £500 in 1968. In 1958, 18 per cent of total gross national product came from agriculture, forestry and fishing. By 1968, the proportion had fallen to 11 per cent although it was two-and-a-half times as great as in 1958. Manufacturing industry, which accounted for 26 per cent of total output in 1958 increased its share to 30 per cent over the same period. Transport, communications and distribution have been reorganized and these service industries account for 25 per cent of gross national product. The proportion of national income devoted to capital investment is now very high, much higher than in Britain or the United States, and this investment is financed by savings. The national resources in Japan devoted to research and development are also growing fast. As a race, the Japanese are eager to make headway and are very willing to study and adopt new techniques of production, management and transport. Over the past decade gross national product per head has grown by an average of about 10 per cent a year. Most of this has occurred in manufacturing industry, where the increase has been much higher. If manpower is switched from, say, agriculture to manufacture, gross national product will thereby be increased, since output per man in manufacturing industry is usually much higher than in agriculture. This switch from industries with a relatively low output per man to those with relatively high output has been the source of much of the economic growth which Japan and other countries at the same stage of development are able to enjoy.

Italy

This country provides another example of rapid development over the past ten years or so, with an average annual growth in gross national product of 5 per cent or more. The take-off stage in the case of Italy was reached a considerable time ago and growth has been helped by a transfer of manpower from agriculture to industry, by a growing rate of capital investment in industry, and the growth of trade in the European Common Market. Italy still has a large production of manpower engaged in agriculture and 13 per cent of gross national product is derived from this source.

Advanced industrial countries

Both Italy and Japan are now on the border-line of the advanced industrial countries. This group has an average gross national product per head of £600–£900. Manufacturing industry contributes an average of 35–40 per cent of total national output, agriculture less than 10 per cent, construction 8 per cent, and transport, communications and distribution 26 per cent. Most of the industrial countries of Western Europe – France, Germany, Belgium, Netherlands, Britain, Norway and Denmark, are within this group. The two latter countries are, however, somewhat exceptional – Norway, with its large merchant fleet derives 18 per cent of national income from transport services; Denmark, with its highly organized factory farming, 14 per cent from agriculture. In general, manufacturing industry provides the fastest growing sector of the economy, and this sector has the highest output per head. Capital investment accounts for an average of about 20 per cent of gross national product. There is some evidence that the countries which have the fastest rate of growth are those which devote the highest proportion of gross national product to investment. Foreign trade is important, and surprising, perhaps, is the fact that these highly industrialized countries buy and sell vast quantities of industrial goods to and from one another.

'Affluent Societies'

Countries with a gross product per head (factor cost) of £1,000 a year are now considered as 'affluent' although this term is sometimes also used concerning some of the more advanced industrial countries. At the head of these is the United States (£1,660 per head), closely followed by Kuwait, an oil-producing country in the Persian Gulf, with Canada, Sweden, Switzerland, Australia, and New Zealand in the £1,000–£1,200 range. Kuwait is exceptional in that a very large proportion of the wealth and income of the country is in the hands of a very few people. Australia obtains a significant share of its national product from mining and agriculture; New Zealand from highly organized farming.

The United States

The proportion of gross national product in the USA obtained from manufacturing industry is lower than in most European countries and the contribution made by the service trades and industries correspondingly higher. Wages and salaries are much higher than in Europe, and the capital equipment available to the American worker together with the power at his elbow are two or three times that available to the British worker. The American economy is a high productivity economy which pays high wages and salaries and makes use of a great deal of capital equipment. As such, it has reached the highest stage of industrial development of any country in the world and the inhabitants of USA have long experienced the benefits of the affluent society. Even so, the output per head in agriculture is not much higher than in Britain and less than one-third of that in the American manufacturing industries. There is, therefore, some possibility of obtaining an increase in gross national product per head by a transfer of labour from agriculture and the services to manufacture. Such a possibility also exists in Britain, but not nearly to the same degree since output per man in the various sectors of the British economy does not differ very much from the average, and employment in agriculture is relatively small.

Population trends

It has already been stated that in many of the poorer countries population is increasing as fast as, or even faster than output. Estimates made of future population suggest that this tendency may continue. These estimates are given below:

	Population Millions	Projected population* Millions	
	1965	1970	1980
Less developed countries	1,500	1,700	2,165
Developed countries	695	725	805
Centrally planned countries	1,075	1,150	1,300
Total	3,270	3,575	4,270

* Still more recent estimates broadly confirm the projected population figures.

The annual rate of increase implied in the 1980 estimate is 2·4 per cent for the less developed countries, 1·0 per cent for the developed countries, and 1·3 per cent for the centrally planned countries (China, Russia, and the Communist bloc). It is doubtful whether output in the less developed countries is increasing, at least at present, as fast as population. Increases in the supply of capital equipment and technical assistance could bring about a significant improvement in output.

Part 2 The Structure of the National Accounts

CHAPTER 4
THE INDUSTRY AND SERVICE ORIGIN OF GROSS NATIONAL PRODUCT

Introduction

In the next few chapters we shall be considering a number of aspects of gross national product by studying the estimates prepared and published by the statisticians in Government service, mainly in the Central Statistical Office. Each year in the early autumn, a comprehensive set of estimates is published as a Blue Book under the title of *National Income and Expenditure, 19—*. The 1969 issue brought the estimates up to the end of 1968. The latest edition of this Blue Book is absolutely indispensible for all students of national account economics. It provides a very wide-ranging assessment of the current economic state of the nation and compares it with that existing over the past fifteen years or so. All the output statistics quoted in this chapter are derived from this source.

As we saw in Chapter 2, national income and national product can be regarded in three ways, since national income equals national expenditure and equals the value of all the goods produced and services rendered over a given period, usually a year. Although we have set down the production valuation as the third of these identities, we shall begin our study with it because it is perhaps the easiest of the three to comprehend.

Gross national product by industry

Table 2 of the 1969 Blue Book is reproduced below as Table 4·1. This shows the contribution to gross domestic product at factor cost of some thirteen broad industrial and service groups over the eleven years 1958–68 inclusive. The footnote to the Table states that this contribution is calculated prior to the deduction of depreciation. This point will be broadly understood by readers, and the question of depreciation will be gone into more fully later in this book. Two new items should, however, be defined at this stage – stock appreciation and residual error.

Table 4.1. Gross national product by industry

£ million

	1958	1959	1960	1961	1962	1963	1964	1965	1966	1967	1968
Agriculture, forestry and fishing	872	877	912	952	988	982	1,024	1,054	1,075	1,129	1,127
Mining and quarrying	713	678	675	695	732	735	737	709	698	700	687
Manufacturing	7,006	7,470	8,198	8,454	8,568	9,068	10,010	10,825	11,106	11,488	12,527
Construction	1,180	1,247	1,374	1,509	1,636	1,740	2,014	2,180	2,295	2,335	2,456
Gas, electricity and water	525	571	618	676	741	837	920	1,035	1,081	1,148	1,288
Transport	1,220	1,293	1,532	1,575	1,636	1,766	1,861	2,004	2,066	2,077	2,266
Communication	377	393	421	448	479	522	580	647	702	751	799
Distributive trades	2,435	2,584	2,771	2,888	3,029	3,192	3,419	3,594	3,771	3,797	4,082
Insurance, banking and finance (including real estate)	568	625	686	780	861	927	976	1,006	1,033	1,145	1,206
Ownership of dwellings	765	835	901	964	1,052	1,149	1,262	1,396	1,521	1,656	1,801
Public administration and defence	1,220	1,262	1,323	1,383	1,459	1,552	1,673	1,801	1,965	2,083	2,258
Public health and educational services	749	822	906	976	1,082	1,184	1,271	1,420	1,565	1,684	1,818
Other services	2,165	2,365	2,569	2,946	3,071	3,351	3,621	3,851	4,141	4,445	4,731
less Stock appreciation	5	—90	—135	—173	—149	—195	—302	—334	—320	—187	—650
Residual error	315	219	—188	66	45	16	—100	—293	—109	135	—129

	1958	1959	1960	1961	1962	1963	1964	1965	1966	1967	£ million 1968
Gross domestic product at factor cost	20,115	21,151	22,563	24,139	25,230	26,826	28,966	30,895	32,590	34,386	36,267
Net property income from abroad	293	260	231	252	333	392	407	469	416	419	419
Gross national product at factor cost	20,408	21,411	22,794	24,391	25,563	27,218	29,373	31,364	33,006	34,805	36,686

* The contribution of each industry to the gross national product before providing for depreciation and stock appreciation.

Stock appreciation

A small part of the output of manufacturing industry, agriculture, and mining is derived from an increase in the values of stocks held by these sectors. Students of accountancy will know that total output is equal to sales plus stock at the end of the trading period minus stock at the beginning. Where stocks are valued at their current prices any increase in such prices will automatically increase the value of these stocks without changing their physical volume. This increase is known as stock appreciation, and is not allowable in the computation of gross national product. Hence a deduction is made for it in the Table. In 1958 this was a tiny addition; prices tended to fall slightly in that year.

Residual Error

The value of gross national product used in this table has been derived from methods of computation other than that of valuing the output of goods and services. To the extent that gross domestic product arrived at from this latter process differs from the one used, the difference – very small in proportion to the total – is used as a balancing factor.

Consideration of contribution of individual sectors

This is perhaps best done by expressing the contribution of each sector as a percentage of gross domestic product. Table 4.2. shows these calculations for the years 1958 and 1968, together with percentage growth over the same period. In this calculation, stock appreciation and residual error have been ignored, but with only a slight loss of accuracy (totals do not add to 100 per cent).

The sectors detailed in Tables 4.1. and 4.2. are generally self-explanatory. It might be pointed out that ownership of dwellings includes rents paid to public authorities, firms and individuals, but also an estimated part in respect of owner-occupied dwellings. The 80 per cent increase in gross domestic product over the decade is at current prices; at constant prices the increase would be about 37 per cent. Sectors of greatest growth have been the provision of gas, electricity, water and public health and educational services (hospitals, schools, colleges, universities, etc.) and ownership of dwellings. At the other end of the scale, mining and quarrying actually declined due, no doubt, to the lessened importance of coal; agriculture increased at less than half the national rate and the distributive trades by four-fifths of the national rate. Manufacturing grew at about the

Table 4 2. Industrial contribution to gross domestic product as a percentage

	Increase per cent 1958–68	Per cent 1958	Contribution 1968	Per cent employment 1968*
Agriculture, forestry and fishing	29·2	4·3	3·1	3·3
Mining and quarrying	−3·6	3·5	1·9	2·1
Manufacturing	78·8	34·8	34·5	35·5
Construction	108·1	5·9	6·8	6·4
Gas, electricity and water	145·3	2·6	3·6	1·7
Transport	85·7	6·1	6·2 ⎫	6·6
Communication	111·9	1·9	2·2 ⎭	
Distributive trades	67·6	12·1	11·3	13·8
Insurance, banking and finance	112·3	2·8	3.3	2·7
Ownership of dwellings	135·4	3·8	5·0	—
Public administration and defence	85·1	6·1	6·2 ⎫	7·4
Public health and educational services	142·7	3.7	5·0 ⎭	
Other services	118·5	10·7	13·0	21·7
Gross domestic product	80·3			

* Estimated – official figures not yet available (mid 1970).

same rate as the distributive trades, services somewhat faster. This is characteristic of the affluent society.

The proportions of gross domestic product contributed by the various sectors in 1968 may come as a surprise to many readers. Together, the extractive industries provide only 5 per cent of total national output. Insurance, banking and finance are more important than agriculture in spite of the fact that a significant part of agricultural output is made up of Government subsidies to farmers. Distribution and other services provide nearly one quarter of national output; manufacturing industry plus gas, water, and electricity, about 38 per cent.

Output per head in the various sectors
If we divide total gross domestic product by total employment we can deduce the average output per head of each employed person. In

1968, the average number of persons in employment was 25,283,000, giving an average output per head of a little less than £1,450. Not all of this can be ascribed to labour; capital, of course, contributes its share and the greater the contribution of capital, the larger output per head tends to be. The final column of table 4.2. shows the distribution of employment in the various sectors. (These employment figures are to be found in Department of Employment and Productivity publications, not in the Blue Book.) If the employment percentage is above the percentage contribution to gross domestic product, output per head is lower than the national average; if below, it is higher.

The differences between percentage contribution and percentage employment are not, on the whole, very startling. Manufacturing industry appears to be slightly worse than average. The gas, water and electricity industries, which are extremely highly capitalized in relation to manpower employed, have an output-per-man ratio double that of the national average. Agriculture and mining are somewhat below average; in the former case about a quarter of the total value of output is accounted for by direct government subsidies. Without these, output per person employed would be only 70 per cent of average. Output per head in mining is kept down by retaining unprofitable mines; if these were all closed output per man would rise significantly (as it has done over the past few years).

In the service trades, distribution is appreciably below average and other services very much below. In the latter case, particularly, the contribution of capital equipment to output is very small – e.g. hairdressers, accountants, and office cleaners. Output per person in the central and local government services is comparatively high. This is because such a large proportion of the members of these groups are highly qualified and well-paid salaried officials.

Method of calculating the contribution to gross domestic product

This method of arriving at gross domestic, and gross national product is essentially one of aggregating output. The contribution of an individual factory to gross domestic product is the value of the work done there. In output terms, it is the total value of sales plus stocks of finished goods minus the value of all materials, parts and services used in producing this output. In other words, it is the 'value added' to the materials, parts and services bought by the factory in unit time, which in this case is usually a year. This principle applies to manufacturing industry as a whole.

However, this kind of calculation is not a very easy one. A close approximation to it is made possible by the periodic full censuses of production, the last three of which were conducted for the years 1958, 1963 and 1968. In these all but the smallest firms in manufacturing industries were asked by the Board of Trade[1] to complete a detailed schedule of their sales, changes in stocks, and purchases, together with wages and salaries paid, numbers on pay roll, and capital expenditure. The results are processed by computer and then the findings for each major industry separately published. Thus, Report No. 48 (there are well over 100) of the 1963 census of production refers to office machinery. It shows, *inter alia*, that sales plus stock changes in 1963 for all firms in the industry totalled £63·435 million; purchases (of listed items), £28·185 million; wages and salaries paid to the 30·2 thousand operatives in the industry, £22·857 million; and capital expenditure, £2·568 million.

The sales plus stock change (£63·435 million) is known as gross output; when the listed purchases are deducted (£28·185 million) the remainder is known as net output or value added. In this case it is £35·250 million. When net output is divided by the number employed, a figure of net output per head is obtained, *viz*, £1,164. The net output per person in the office machinery industry is very low, one reason for which is that the capital expenditure and capital stock per worker is low. In some highly capitalized sectors of the chemical industry, the net output per person is well over £2,000.

Net output is more or less synonymous with the contribution to gross domestic product; it is usually a little higher than this contribution since all the firms' and industries' purchases are not listed. Nevertheless, the statisticians who compute the national accounts make great use of the basic data provided by the census of production. From the 130 or so reports for 1963, the student can discover how great is the variation in output per person employed in manufacturing. The 1968 census results will not be ready in detail for some time yet; but provisional results have already been published (see Appendix IV).

But these censuses of production returns cover only manufacturing industry. In the service trades, distribution, the professions, and central and local government service, it is not possible to calculate the output by direct measurement, since it is in the form of work, not goods. Hence the contribution made by these groups must be

---

[1] Now this is done by the Business Statistics Office.

assessed in a different way. And here we see once more the essential unity of the three ways of calculating gross national or domestic product. The production of goods and services yields an income to those concerned in providing them – and the total income thus obtained must equal the total value of the goods and services produced (profits being properly regarded as income to the firm and its owners).

Table 17 in the 1969 Blue Book – gross domestic product by industry and type of income – gives the detailed composition of the contribution of each sector, by way of the income approach. Two examples will suffice; manufacturing industry and public administration and defence.

Table 4.3. Income approach to contribution to gross domestic product 1968

	Manufacturing	£'s million Public administration and defence
Wages	5,248	493
Salaries	2,765	915
Pay in cash and kind. H.M. Forces	–	542
Employers' contributions to social security	697	308
Total income from employment	8,710	2,258
Gross profits of companies and trading surplus of public corporations	3,620	—
Income from self-employment and other income	197	—
Total	12,527	2,258

These totals agree with the ones shown in table 4.1. The sources of the detailed figures are varied, and the compilation of the totals is a triumph of ingenuity and skill on the part of the compilers. Just as the full census of production is of great help in arriving at the contribution of manufacturing industry, so the occasional census of distribution assists in the assessment of the contribution of distribution. Regular information on wage rates and earnings produced by the Department of Employment and Productivity, and analyses of wages, salaries, and profits produced by the Inland Revenue departments all assist in the assessment process.

There is one very important difference between the make-up of the figures in the two columns shown in 4.3. to which attention should be drawn. In the public administration and defence column, all the income comes from employment, wages, salaries, pay of H.M. forces, etc. Profits or trading surpluses by their very nature can play no part in the total contribution to gross domestic product. This means that the output of those engaged in public administration and defence always equals the salaries or wages received, and productivity increases can only accrue from the receipt of successive increments in a progressive salary, or by promotion to a higher grade carrying an increased remuneration. If all civil service salaries are increased by, say, 5 per cent, productivity is unaffected, since in national income account conventions it is merely a price increase unaccompanied by an increase in output.

CHAPTER 5
GROSS NATIONAL PRODUCT CONSIDERED AS THE SUM OF FACTOR INCOMES

Introduction

In Chapter 4 the gross national product was stated as the total, expressed in money terms, of the output of all industries and services. But, as we have already seen (and this cannot be emphasized too much) output and incomes must equal one another. In this chapter, therefore, we are considering the incomes side of the identity. Table 5.1. shows these totals for the period 1958 to 1968. The term factor incomes is used because the incomes which are distinguished are related to the factors of production: labour, capital, and land. The three main types of income distinguished in Table 5.1. are incomes from employment, i.e. payments to labour; gross trading profits of companies and public enterprises, i.e. the return for the use of capital; and rent, the return for the use of land and buildings not already included in the return for the use of capital. Perhaps we could pause a moment and look at the definition of rent as given in the Blue Book.

Rent is defined thus: gross receipts from ownership of land and buildings, less actual expenditure by the owners on repairs, maintenance, and insurance. An imputed income from owner-occupied trading and industrial property is included in trading income. The meaning of imputed income will be discussed later (Chapter 7).

The composition of, and trends in, factor incomes

Again, it will be convenient if the various factor incomes are expressed as a percentage of gross national product. This has been done in table 5.2., and in this section tables 5.1. and 5.2. should be considered together. But first there are two further terms appearing in these tables which must now be defined more closely, namely, capital consumption and national income.

The factor incomes are calculated (as is the gross, national product by industry) 'before providing for depreciation' where this is appropriate; for example, in the case of trading profits of various kinds and also in the case of rent. These profits are not true profits in the sense that provision has not been made for maintaining capital equipment at its value at the beginning of the year. Plant and machinery deteriorate as a result of use. This deterioration, sometimes known as wear and tear, is, for obvious reasons, of more importance in the case of plant and machinery than buildings: the latter may last many years, the former only a few. The estimated value of wear and tear in a year is called capital consumption in the national accounts. Conventionally, capital consumption in these accounts is equated with depreciation or the sums set aside for maintaining capital intact. The experts calculate it by applying the statutory tax allowances for income tax and corporation tax to estimates of capital stock. Conventionally, but also conceptually correct, the sums set aside for maintaining capital intact, or by way of depreciation, are regarded as not being available for factor incomes. Gross trading profits, as quoted in table 5.1., are arrived at before this allowance is made. The balance of gross national product after all depreciation allowances have been deducted is known as national income. It is therefore that part, currently about 91 per cent, of gross national product which is available for factor incomes.

Incomes from employment and from self-employment present few conceptual difficulties to the student of economics but they include pensions. Gross trading profits less depreciation can without undue sophistication be regarded as income to the owners of companies, public corporations, or other public enterprises. Rent has already been defined.

Public corporations, in general, are the nationalized industries – coal, gas, water, and electricity, rail and air transport, post office, etc., and from time to time, iron and steel and parts of the road transport industry. The two latter have been nationalized, denationalized, and renationalized over the period covered by the statistics in table 5.2., depending upon the Government in power. The small item of gross trading surplus of other public enterprises includes the Post Office Savings Bank, the commercial activity of the Atomic Energy Authority (for some of the time), and the activities of certain specialized bodies such as the National Film Finance Corporation and the National Research and Development Corporation.

Over the 20 years from 1948 to 1968, gross national product grew from £10,517 million to £36,586 million; an increase of 250 per cent at current prices. This increase represents an average annual increase of nearly 6·5 per cent in money terms. The change in the proportion of gross national product obtained by the various factors over this

Table 5.1. Gross national product by factor incomes

£ million

	1958	1959	1960	1961	1962	1963	1964	1965	1966	1967	1968
Factor incomes											
Income from employment	13,470	14,107	15,174	16,407	17,307	18,191	19,703	21,261	22,741	23,615	25,267
Income from self-employment*	1,786	1,890	2,014	2,117	2,155	2,215	2,342	2,527	2,665	2,772	2,840
Gross trading profits of companies*	2,983	3,317	3,736	3,643	3,595	4,108	4,601	4,778	4,455	4,637	5,117
Gross trading surplus of public corporations*	340	391	539	645	751	846	931	995	1,049	1,139	1,352
Gross trading surplus of other public enterprises*	155	164	179	96	71	78	91	96	87	92	111
Rent†	1,061	1,153	1,244	1,338	1,455	1,567	1,700	1,865	2,022	2,183	2,359
Total domestic income before providing for depreciation and stock appreciation	19,795	21,022	22,886	24,246	25,334	27,005	29,368	31,522	33,019	34,438	37,046
less Stock appreciation	5	—90	—135	—173	—149	—195	—302	—334	—320	—187	—65
Residual error	315	219	—188	66	45	16	—100	—293	—109	135	—129

	1958	1959	1960	1961	1962	1963	1964	1965	1966	1967	£ million 1968
Gross domestic product at factor cost	20,115	21,151	22,563	24,139	25,230	26,826	28,966	30,895	32,590	34,386	36,267
Net property income from abroad	293	260	231	252	333	392	407	469	416	419	419
Gross national product	20,408	21,411	22,794	24,391	25,563	27,218	29,373	31,364	33,006	34,805	36,686
Capital consumption	1,791	1,844	1,933	2,065	2,197	2,318	2,492	2,697	2,937	3,148	3,375
National income	18,617	19,567	20,861	22,326	23,366	24,900	26,881	28,667	30,069	31,657	33,311

* Before providing for depreciation and stock appreciation
† Before providing for depreciation

Table 5.2. Gross national product. Percentage distribution by factor incomes

	1948	1953	1958	1959	1960	1961	1962	1963	1964	1965	1966	1967	1968	1938
Income from employment	64·5	64·0	66·0	65·9	66·6	67·3	67·7	66·8	67·1	67·8	68·9	67·8	68·9	58·4
Income from self employment	12·4	10·2	8·8	8·8	8·8	8·7	8·4	8·1	8·0	8·1	8·1	8·0	7·7	12·5
Gross trading profits of companies	17·0	15·4	14·6	15·5	16·4	14·9	14·1	15·1	15·6	15·2	13·5	13·3	13·9	13·3
Gross trading surplus of public corporations*	1·1	2·1	1·7	1·8	2·4	2·6	2·9	3·1	3·2	3·2	3·2	3·3	3·7	0·2
Gross trading surplus of other public enterprises*	1·0	0·4	0·8	0·8	0·8	0·4	0·3	0·3	0·3	0·3	0·3	0·3	0·3	1·2
Rent*	4·3	4·5	5·2	5·4	5·5	5·5	5·7	5·8	5·8	5·9	6·1	6·3	6·4	9·1
Less Stock Appreciation	−3·1	+0·5	–	−0·4	−0·6	−0·7	−0·6	−0·7	−1·0	−1·1	−1·0	−0·6	−1·8	1·5
Residual error	0·5	1·5	1·5	1·0	−0·8	0·3	0·2	–	−0·3	−0·9	−0·3	0·4	−0·4	–
GDP at factor cost	97·8	98·5	98·6	98·8	99·0	99·0	98·7	98·6	98·6	98·5	98·7	98·8	98·9	96·3
Net property income from abroad	2·2	1·5	1·4	1·2	1·0	1·0	1·3	1·4	1·4	1·5	1·3	1·2	1·1	3·7
GNP	100·0	100·0	100·0	100·0	100·0	100·0	100·0	100·0	100·0	100·0	100·0	100·0	100·0	100·0
Capital consumption	8·1	8·6	8·8	8·6	8·5	8·5	8·6	8·5	8·5	8·6	8·9	9·0	9·2	6·9
National income	91·9	91·4	91·2	91·4	91·5	91·5	91·4	91·5	91·5	91·4	91·1	91·0	90·8	93·1

*Before providing for depreciation.

period has, however, not been very great but certain trends are unmistakable. There has been a persistent tendency for income from employment to obtain a larger share of gross national product. Over the 15 years from 1953 to 1968, the percentage share taken by income from employment rose from 64·0 to 68·9. An increase of this magnitude must mean that employees have increased their living standards at a slightly faster rate than the rest of the community. This increase in the proportion of gnp accruing to employees has been more than offset by the fall in the proportion received by self-employed persons and by way of gross trading profits of companies. Part of the fall in the former can be ascribed to a fall in the numbers of professional persons, farmers, and other sole traders and partnerships. Competition from large stores has certainly reduced the number of small shopkeepers. The fall in the share received by gross trading profits of companies may be partly caused by the higher proportion taken by employees. No doubt, too, public corporations which have increased their share of gnp from 2·1 per cent to 3·7 per cent over the 1953–68 period, have encroached more and more on the field formerly held by private enterprise companies. Rent, too, has steadily increased its share – not so much by higher rents paid by tenants as from the imputed rents on the rapidly growing stock of owner-occupied dwellings. Capital consumption has taken a slowly growing share of gross national product; capital stock may well be growing faster than gross national product.

Income from employment appears to be less susceptible to the prevailing economic conditions than do gross trading profits of companies. The fall in the share of gnp obtained by way of trading profits of companies has fallen noticeably since 1965; the economic squeeze began in the middle of 1966 and was in full force throughout 1967, 1968, and 1969. The share going to income from employment has grown quite noticeably during this period. Other years of slow economic growth have been 1952, 1956, 1958, and 1961–62. The three latter years were poor years for trading profits but good years for income from employment.

Comparison with 1938

And finally let us draw a comparison with 1938, the last full year before the outbreak of the Second World War. The first half of 1938 showed a decline in economic activity compared with 1937 but the growing effort on rearmament brought about a resumption of economic growth in the second half. There were over 1,800,000 persons unemployed in June 1938. Naturally, therefore, income from employment was a much lower proportion of gross national product (58·4 per cent), for not only was there a large number of unemployed receiving no income from employment, but their existence weakened the bargaining power of trade unions. Income from self-employment equalled 12·5 per cent of gross national product – unemployment did not unduly affect this. Gross trading profit of companies was exactly the same proportion as in 1967. Public corporations, as such, hardly existed, but the Post Office was then regarded as a public enterprise. Rent attracted over 9 per cent of gross national product largely because rents of dwelling houses were more economic than now. Although 1938 showed a slight deficit on balance of payments, income from abroad was a relatively more important element in the economy than today. Capital consumption was lower because the national capital stock was very much lower.

Constituents of income from employment

Income from employment is broken down into a number of its constituent elements in a table which shows income and expenditure in the personal sector. Table 5.3. gives this analysis for 1958 and 1968.

Table 5.3. Analysis of income from employment

| | £ million | |
	1958	1968
Wages	7,795	12,860
Salaries	4,340	9,590
Pay in cash and kind of H.M. Forces	395	542
Employers' contributions:		
National insurance etc.	398	1,102
Other (pensions, redundancy payments, etc.)	542	1,173
Total income from employment	13,470	25,267
Professional persons	294	502
Farmers	448	640
Other sole traders and partnerships	1,044	1,698
Total income from self-employment	1,786	2,840

There are a number of points on the above table which call for comment. Wages increased by 65 per cent between 1958 and 1960 but salaries by 110 per cent. Unfortunately, there are no complete statistics which show the total number of employees divided into wage and salary earners. A table in the Blue Book estimates these numbers for manufacturing industries as a whole; employees in manufacturing are roughly one third of the total in employment. Between 1958 and 1968 the numbers of wage earners in manufacturing fell from 6,110,000 to 5,685,000 but the number of salary earners rose from 1,650,000 to 2,070,000. This tendency for the proportion of salary earners to increase is not restricted to manufacturing industries but is a common feature of industrial development. Office work, partly on account of legislation such as PAYE, Selective Employment Tax, etc., has grown steadily over the past 20 years. There is a small but growing tendency for wage earners to be granted salary-earning status. In 1958 salary earners in manufacturing represented 21·3 per cent of all employees and the average salary earned was £790 per annum. Ten years later the proportion was 26·7 per cent with an average salary of £1,335. Over this same period average wages grew from £525 to £925. In ten years average salaries grew by 70 per cent, average wages by 76 per cent – not much difference over ten years.

The great improvement in service pay and conditions over the past decade is shown by the fact that the average value of these rose from £645 per person in 1958 to £1,350 in 1968. Farmers' earnings did not keep pace with the general trends, but those of professional persons and other sole traders and partnerships may well have done so.

Sources of information on factor incomes

As pointed out already, it is part of the expertise of an experienced economic statistician to cast his net widely and combine disparate sources of information into a unified whole. Returns made to the Department of Employment and Productivity and Inland Revenue authorities (from both individuals and companies) are perhaps the main sources. The accounts of public corporations must, of course, be published and the financial transactions of government departments (including Ministry of Defence) shown in the Appropriation Accounts. The *Employment and Productivity Gazette*, together with kindred publications by the Department of Employment and Productivity, contains a great deal of regular information on earnings and employment which is the basis of wage incomes. Rent income is arrived at from Schedule D tax assessments; imputed income from rateable values are arrived at with the help of the Family Expenditure Survey (about which more will be said later).

CHAPTER 6
GROSS NATIONAL PRODUCT CONSIDERED FROM THE POINT OF VIEW OF EXPENDITURE

Introduction

We now turn to the third main approach to the gross national product. namely, expenditure. In this approach we consider the components of total expenditure which we divide into consumers' expenditure; current expenditure by the government and other public authorities; expenditure by way of capital investment by the government, public authorities, companies and individuals; expenditure by other countries on the goods and services made in this country which is offset against this country's expenditure on goods and services from abroad; and expenditure which goes into the building-up of stocks and work-in-progress.

At the outset, the link between expenditure and incomes is again brought to the attention of students. Expenditure on the part of individuals, firms, and public authorities must lead to incomes on the part of individuals and institutions in these sectors. The one exception to this is that imported goods are paid for by British nationals but the increased incomes which follow accrue to the nationals of other countries. Conversely, exports from Britain generate incomes in this country by way of expenditure in other countries. The closeness of the association of expenditure and incomes used to be emphasized in the relevant table in the Blue Book by its sub-title, 'Expenditure generating gross national product'.

Gross national product at market prices

However, when we try to equate expenditure and factor incomes we immediately run up against a difficulty. When anyone buys a packet of cigarettes or a bottle of spirits, the whole of the expenditure involved is part of consumer's expenditure. But only a relatively small portion of the price paid by the purchaser finds its way into factor incomes or rewards paid for the use of the labour, capital, natural resources and enterprise involved in the production of the articles in question. The bulk of the cost of cigarettes and spirits is made up of taxation which goes to the central government as a levy and not in return for any direct service.

On the other hand, when the consumer buys home-produced food-stuffs, he may well pay less than the total of factor incomes generated by his purchase. This is because the government makes up the difference between what the purchaser pays and the amounts received by those who produce the food by subsidies paid to producers. The price which the final purchaser pays is known as the market price, and, in total, gross national product at market prices is greater than at factor cost by the value of taxes on expenditure less subsidies paid to producers. In 1968, taxes on expenditure amounted to nearly £7,000 million, whilst subsidies (not all to agriculture by any means) reached a figure of £900 million. Hence, gross national product at market prices in 1968 was about one-sixth higher than at factor cost.

In Britain, taxes on expenditure are based in the main on goods and services paid for by the consumer, purchase tax, excise duties and selective employment tax on services. There is little or no taxation on goods and services bought by firms for investment or production. On the Continent, where value-added taxation is common, a proportion of this tax falls on investment and industrial goods – for example, plant and machinery, parts and accessories.

Components of gross national product from the expenditure aspect
Table 6.1. shows gross national product arrived at in this way for the decade 1958–1968. A short description of these components is given below; more detailed explanations follow in later chapters.

Consumers' expenditure. This is the largest of the four or five items which go to make up gross national expenditure. It calls for very little explanation; the Blue Book defines it as 'expenditure on consumers' goods and services by persons and non-profit making bodies, plus the value of incomes in kind'. All business expenditure reckoned as current costs of production is, so far as possible, excluded. The Family Expenditure Survey has been designed to provide figures for the total and categorized expenditure by consumers. This survey has now been in operation for some time and it is giving very reliable results. It is supplemented by information on the numbers of rented and owner-occupied houses from the latest population census – to arrive at a total of rent, rates, water charges, maintenance and repairs to property. The latest census of distribution provides much useful confirmatory

Table 6.1. Gross national product analysed by types of expenditure

	1958	1959	1960	1961	1962	1963	1964	1965	1966	1967	1968
Expenditure											
Consumers' expenditure	15,296	16,106	16,909	17,810	18,906	20,125	21,493	22,865	24,236	25,339	27,065
Public authorities' current expenditure on goods and services	3,750	4,001	4,248	4,589	4,920	5,184	5,512	6,043	6,572	7,246	7,702
Gross domestic fixed capital formation	3,492	3,736	4,120	4,619	4,731	4,916	5,854	6,303	6,707	7,262	7,798
Value of physical increase in stocks and work in progress	111	174	595	323	69	219	654	416	253	202	204
Total domestic expenditure at market prices	22,649	24,017	25,872	27,341	28,626	30,444	33,513	35,627	37,768	40,049	42,869
Exports and property income from abroad	5,839	6,016	6,309	6,587	6,840	7,225	7,693	8,312	8,749	8,893	10,670
less Imports and property income paid abroad	—5,425	—5,791	—6,483	—6,480	—6,607	—6,964	—7,888	—8,153	—8,456	—8,926	—10,679
less Taxes on expenditure	—3,040	—3,200	—3,391	—3,643	—3,896	—4,047	—4,455	—4,986	—5,611	—6,002	—6,960
Subsidies	385	369	487	586	600	560	510	564	556	791	886
Gross national product at factor cost	20,408	21,411	22,794	24,391	25,563	27,218	29,373	31,364	33,006	34,805	36,686

information on the sales of such commodities as are bought only by consumers from a relatively limited number of outlets – clothing, furniture, floor coverings, radio and television sets, for example. The Family Expenditure Survey is taken at regular intervals, the censuses at quite infrequent ones. Even the 'Survey' cannot provide really up-to-date information because of the time required to analyse it. Monthly retail sales figures collected and analysed by the Board of Trade[1] provide the basis for the most up-to-date assessments of consumers' expenditure.

Public authorities' current expenditure on goods and services. The word 'current' here implies non-capital and the expenditure is in respect of goods and services paid for by the Government, local authorities and public bodies. Pensions are by definition excluded; they are transfer payments and not in return for services rendered. The bulk of this item is, in fact, wages and salaries paid to government and local authority employees including the armed forces. The largest single item is military defence (over £2,000 million), followed by education and the national health service. Expenditure on the maintenance of existing goods is included but expenditure on new roads is part of gross fixed investment; likewise, teachers' salaries and the cost of maintaining schools are part of current expenditure, but the cost of building new schools is capital expenditure.

Gross domestic fixed capital formation. The reader is presumed to understand the difference between current and capital expenditure. Current expenditure, briefly, is all expenditure by consumers and that by the public sector on the purchase of services or non-durable goods. Fixed capital formation means expenditure on fixed assets – buildings, vehicles, plant, and machinery, etc. – either for replacing or adding to the stock of existing assets. Such expenditure is often thought of as being in aid of production; factories and their equipment are clearly intended for that purpose. But private dwelling-houses and prisons are regarded as fixed assets; capital expenditure of this kind may have very little effect on production. Capital expenditure in the shape of new roads, bridges, and schools can be seen to have an indirect effect on production. The criterion common to these various types of capital expenditure is that they produce fixed and durable assets.

---

[1] Now the Department of Trade and Industry

Value of physical increase in stocks and work-in-progress. This is the increase in the quantity of stocks and work-in-progress held by trading enterprises and public authorities valued at average prices of the year. It represents expenditure on production prior to final sale. The point has already been made that for trading account purposes, sales are added to the increase in stocks and work-in-progress to give total accounting sales. But no element of price increase is allowed in valuing stocks; this element has been discussed under 'stock appreciation'.

Exports and Imports. These call for no explanatory comment except that they include both goods and services.

Taxes on expenditure. These are of two kinds; central government taxes on expenditure such as purchase tax and excise duty, and those levied by local authorities in the form of rates. This latter item might seem a little out of place but a little thought will show that rates increase the cost of housing services in the same way that purchase tax increases the cost of a washing machine; the extra charge does not go to the provider of the service but to the local authorities.

Subsidies. These are defined in the Blue Book as payments made to a producer or trader with the object of reducing his selling price below the factor cost of production. Agricultural subsidies are the best example of these straight subsidies. But to the extent that a nationalized industry provides services at less than their economic cost and the consequent deficit is made up by the Exchequer, these are also subsidies. British Railways and the National Coal Board have often been subsidized in this way. Local authorities often let their houses at an uneconomic rent and the deficit, if cleared by the Exchequer, must also rank as a subsidy.

Sources of information on the expenditure components of gross national product. These sources, in relation to consumers' expenditure (by far the largest item), have been dealt with already. As all Government expenditure must be scrupulously audited against the amounts voted by Parliament, this expenditure can be found in the Appropriation Accounts of the relevant Government department. In addition, votes and expenditure are also recorded under an 'economic' classification and this is the main source of information on current expenditure on goods and services. Likewise, the receipts from taxes on expenditure are shown in the Annual Report of H.M. Customs and Excise, and subsidies paid by the central government are found in the consolidated statement of government expenditure using an economic classification which is produced annually. Local authority expenditure is also carefully audited and published.

Gross domestic fixed capital formation. This includes government, local authority, and nationalized industries' capital expenditure as well as that of statutory and private companies and private individuals. The 'public sector' element in the total is to be found in the 'economic classification' returns, the annual reports of the nationalized industries, and in returns made to the Department of the Environment by local authorities. 'Private sector' capital expenditure figures are collected quarterly by the Board of Trade (now the Department of Trade and Industry) from most large industrial, commercial, and financial undertakings in Britain, and from a sample of smaller ones. The census of production provides a total figure for industrial undertakings and quarterly changes in capital expenditure can be linked to this total figure.

Stocks and work-in-progress. The information on these is also collected quarterly by the Board of Trade from a similar list of firms but, of course, wholesalers and merchants need to be included.

Trends in expenditure. The percentage distribution of expenditure under the four main headings, at market prices, is given below for five years during the period 1938 to 1968.

Table 6.2. Percentage distribution of expenditure at market prices

	1938	1948	1958	1963	1968
Consumers' expenditure	75½	72	67½	66	63¼
Public authorities' current expenditure	13½	14¾	16½	17	18
Gross domestic fixed capital	11	11¾	15½	16	18¼
Value of physical increase in stocks	–	1½	½	1	½
Total domestic expenditure at market prices	100	100	100	100	100

The most important changes in the distribution of expenditure between 1938 and 1968 have been the reduction in the proportion of consumers' expenditure and the growth in that of capital expenditure and Government and local authority expenditure. The total consumers' expenditure divided by the population, or, consumers' expenditure per head, is the best measure of living standards. The comparatively low gross domestic product in 1938 was offset, so far as these standards are concerned, by the higher proportion going to consumers. Of course, some of the public authorities' current expenditure can be thought of as helping living standards – for example, health and education: defence, although an absolute necessity, does not do so. Clearly, too, the greater the proportion of gnp which is devoted to gross domestic fixed capital formation – or capital expenditure – the smaller the proportion which is left for consumers' expenditure. But capital expenditure is vital to future growth and expansion; the countries with the highest proportion of gross national product devoted to capital expenditure are often the fastest growing countries – Japan and Germany, for example. Capital expenditure necessitates the foregoing of some present satisfaction in order to ensure better living standards in the future. It is satisfactory to see that Britain's share has risen from 11 per cent in 1938 to 18·25 in 1968 but it is still one of the lowest of the main industrial countries, and consumers' expenditure still takes a higher proportion of total production of goods and services than it does in most of these countries. These points are discussed at greater length in a later chapter.

Taxes on expenditure and subsidies are both at a higher comparative level now than in pre-war days. Expressed as a proportion of gross national product at factor cost, taxes on expenditure have risen from 12 to 17 per cent, and subsidies from 0·7 per cent to 1·7 per cent. These figures are a reflection of the higher level of taxation which is now in operation compared with pre-war days and even with a decade ago, and of changes in government policy regarding subsidies. The level of these varies, however, from time to time; they were particularly high in 1962 when support to agriculture by way of subsidies was exceptionally high.

Available resources and their allocation

Finally, in order to emphasize once more the expenditure-income identity, table 6.3. shows total resources and their allocation as the two sides of an account. Total resources are made up of income by way of gross national product at factor cost, and indirect taxes and local rates. To these are added imports of goods and services. On the other side of the account are shown the manner in which these total resources are used – on public expenditure, consumers' expenditure, investment, stock-building, exports, etc.

Table 6.3. Total resources and their allocation

	£ million				£ million	
	1958	1968			1958	1968
Gross national product at factor cost	20,408	36,686		Exports and income received from abroad	5,839	10,670
Imports and income paid overseas	5,425	10,679		Public authorities' current expenditure on goods and services	3,750	7,702
Indirect taxes and local rates	3,040	6,960		Subsidies	385	886
				Gross domestic capital formation		
				(a) fixed investment	3,492	7,798
				(b) increase in value of stocks	106	854
				Personal consumption	15,296	27,065
Total available resources at market prices				Less stock, appreciation	+5	—650
	28,873	54,325			28,873	54,325

The reader should identify the items appearing in the above table with those shown in table 6.1. and in earlier tables.

CHAPTER 7
NOMINAL AND REAL GROWTH IN NATIONAL INCOME AND EXPENDITURE

Introduction

So far, we have discussed the components of national income and expenditure in terms of current prices, that is, the prices ruling in the year to which the figures refer. Thus in table 6.3. the gross national product at factor cost is given as £20,408 million in 1958, and £36,686 million in 1968. These were the estimated totals at prices ruling in 1958 and 1968 respectively. The nominal increase in gross national product between the two dates is almost 80 per cent, or an average annual increase of 6 per cent.[1] At the same time, consumers' expenditure increased by 77 per cent, or just under 6 per cent a year. Those of us who have spent the whole or part of our adult lives in this particular decade know full well that the average standard of living of the people in Britain has not risen by 77 per cent between the two dates. For one thing, there were more people to share in consumers' expenditure in 1968 than ten years earlier. Allowing for this increase in population, the growth in nominal consumption per head was just over 65 per cent, representing an average annual increase of 5·25 per cent. But this does not affect the national increase in consumers' expenditure.

However, the growth in the national standard of living is not really measured by the growth in expenditure on consumers' goods but by the growth in the volume of consumers' goods which this increased expenditure has made possible. And this is where price changes come into the picture. If between 1958 and 1968 the average prices of consumers' goods had risen by 77 per cent, the average standard of living would have remained unchanged; the whole of the increase in expenditure would have been swallowed up by higher prices. In the same way, the real growth in gross national product is represented by the growth in the volume of goods and services produced, not by the increase in their monetary value,

---

[1] For method of calculating growth rates, see Appendix III.

This is not to say that national income and expenditure accounts expressed at current prices have little value; far from it. It is quite in order to express the components of gross national product as a proportion of the total using current prices in each case as in table 6.2. Moreover, if the increase in the volume of imports and exports over a period is the same but export prices have risen faster than import prices, then there has been a real gain to this country on account of a favourable movement in the terms of trade. Numerous other examples of the use of the national accounts at current prices will no doubt occur to the reader. Economic growth is, however, generally assessed in volume, or real terms.

Price indices of the gross national product and its components

Whilst it must be true that the real growth in consumption or gross national product is represented by the additional goods and services consumed by the people, or produced by the nation as a whole, it is quite impossible to measure these increases or put a value on them. The best that can be done is to assess the increase, expressed in money terms, in consumption or gross national product as a whole, and remove from these increases the effect of price changes. In practice, the effect of price changes is removed from the separate components of gross national product and the aggregate effect then represents the price change in gross national product as a whole. This is done by the use of price index numbers.

We have seen in earlier chapters that the gross national product can be arrived at by summing the output of all industries and services, by summing the incomes of individuals and corporate bodies, and, as in the immediately preceding chapter, by summing total expenditure under a number of headings such as consumption and investment. The first and the third methods, in particular, lend themselves to the use of price index numbers as correcting factors for price changes. By way of illustration, reference is made to the table in the 1969 Blue Book dealing with index numbers of costs and prices. The price indices section of this table shows the following:

Table 7.1. Index numbers of prices – components of gross national products (1963 = 100)

	1958	1959	1960	1961	1962	1963	1964	1965	1966	1967	1968
Consumer goods and services	89·9	90·8	91·8	94·5	98·2	100·0	103·2	108·0	112·1	115·0	120·0
Fixed assets	93	93	93	95	98	100	102	106	110	111	115
All final goods and services sold on the home market	89·1	90·2	91·6	94·4	97·8	100·0	103·3	108·2	112·7	115·9	120·9
Exports of goods and services	96	96	97	98	99	100	101	103	106	109	118
Total final output	90·2	91·2	92·4	94·9	97·9	100·0	103·0	107·4	111·6	114·7	120·4
Imports of goods and services	96	97	98	98	98	100	103	104	106	107	119

It is presumed that the reader has some knowledge of the purpose and composition of the more important price index numbers now being calculated and published in Britain. At the time of writing, these index numbers are based on 1963=100. The year 1963 was a year for which the quinquennial Census of Production was carried out, and this inquiry provided a great deal of information for the calculation of indices of industrial production which were then re-based on 1963, some time during 1969. (Previously they had been based on 1958=100.) Most index numbers of wholesale prices were thereupon recalculated to a 1963 base in order to keep them in line with index numbers of industrial production.

The index numbers shown in table 7.1. and in the 1969 Blue Book are composite index numbers formed by combining a larger number of separate index numbers. The price index number for consumer goods and services is calculated in much the same way and from much the same information as the index of retail prices which is a composite index derived from many individual series. However, in national income price index numbers, the weighting system used always re-lates to the year in question – for 1968 the consumer goods and ser-vices index uses 1968 weights; the index of retail prices uses weights representative of a somewhat earlier period. The price index number for fixed assets is likewise built up from many individual series – 15 different indices are calculated for plant and machinery alone. The calculation of individual and composite indices to measure changes in building costs is particularly difficult. For further information on these topics the reader is referred to *National Accounts Statistics – Sources and Methods* (1968 edition).

Table 7.1. in showing that the price index for consumer goods and services rose from 89·9 in 1958 to 120·0 in 1968, implies that prices of these goods and services rose by 33·5 per cent between 1958 and 1968. It has already been pointed out that consumers' expenditure rose by 77 per cent during the same period. The real increase in this expendi-ture over the ten years is calculated thus:

(1) Consumers' expenditure in 1968, as a percentage of 1958,

$$= \frac{£27,065}{£15,296} \text{ m} \times 100 = 176\cdot9 \text{ per cent}$$

(2) Price index for consumers' goods etc. in 1968, as a percentage,

$$= \frac{120\cdot0}{89\cdot9} \times 100 = 133\cdot5$$

(3) 'Real' or volume level of consumers' expenditure 1968, as a percentage of 1958,

$$= \frac{176 \cdot 9}{133 \cdot 5} \times 100 = 132 \cdot 5 \text{ per cent}$$

(4) Real increase in consumers' expenditure between 1958 and 1968 = 32·5 per cent

Revaluation of the components of gross national product at 1963 prices
The tables in the Blue Book giving expenditure and output in real terms do so by expressing these various components at constant 1963 prices. Thus, consumers' expenditure in 1958 and 1968 at 1963 prices is given as £17,008 million and £22,562 million respectively; Gross national product at market prices, £25,886 million and £35,429 million, respectively. Consumers' expenditure revalued at 1963 prices is obtained by applying the price index numbers for this expenditure for 1958 and 1968 based on 1963 = 100.
Thus:

	1958	1968
(i) Consumers' expenditure, current prices	£15,296 m.	£27,065 m.
(ii) Consumers' expenditure, price index	89·9	120·0
(iii)Consumers' expenditure, constant 1963 prices	£17,010 m.	£22,560 m.

(iii) is obtained from (i) by dividing by the price index and multiplying by 100. The student should calculate for himself consumers' expenditure and gross domestic fixed capital say, for the years 1958 to 1968 at constant 1963 prices, and compare his results with those given in the Blue Book. Incidentally, it will be noted that the increase between 1958 and 1968 in consumers' expenditure at constant 1963 prices is 32·5 per cent – the result obtained in the previous paragraph.

The contribution to gross domestic product at 1963 prices by the various industries and services is shown in the Blue Book as percentages of 1963 = 100; agriculture, forestry and fishing being 84 in 1958, and 112 in 1968, for example. It is convenient to do this because, as we have already said, industrial output is usually calculated as an index based on a census of production year – e.g. 1963. Many of these indices are calculated regularly for incorporation in the index of industrial production, and they can be fed straight into the national accounts. Thus, the index for manufacturing is produced monthly by the Central Statistical Office, and annual figures are used in the national accounts – 83·3 for 1958, 121·2 for 1968, with 1963 =

100. In the first place, the index of production for manufacturing industry is obtained by applying appropriate price index numbers to output valued at current prices – i.e., the principle illustrated in the previous section is followed exactly.

Gross national product at constant prices
A range of figures for each of the years from 1948 to 1968 is shown in the 1969 Blue Book, for gross national product, gross domestic

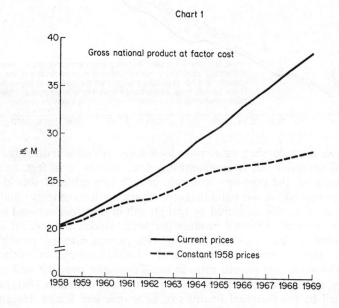

Chart 1

product and net national product. These are indices based on 1963 = 100 and are also expressed as values at 1963 prices. From either of these sets of figures, the real growth in national output can be directly obtained. Chart 1 shows gross national product at factor cost both at current and constant 1958 prices from 1958 to 1969. Chart 2 shows gross national product as an index (1963 = 100) for gross national product at constant prices from 1948 to 1969.

The latter indicates that gross national product at factor cost rose from an index level of 67·1 in 1948 to 114·7 in 1968. This is an increase of 71 per cent in 20 years, or an average of nearly 2·75 per cent a year.

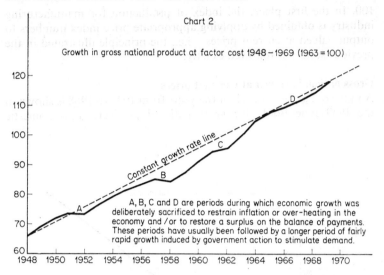

Chart 2

Growth in gross national product at factor cost 1948 – 1969 (1963 = 100)

A, B, C and D are periods during which economic growth was deliberately sacrificed to restrain inflation or over-heating in the economy and / or to restore a surplus on the balance of payments. These periods have usually been followed by a longer period of fairly rapid growth induced by government action to stimulate demand.

As we shall see when we come to look at growth rates in other industrial countries this is comparatively low. Britain is, in fact, at the bottom of the post-war economic growth rate table. It should be re-emphasised at this point that economic growth, as generally understood, is usually measured by real growth in the gross national product, or gross national product per head. Hence, the student and general reader should be familiar with current rates of growth in gross national product in Britain and her main industrial competitors.

For economic growth rates in these countries over the past century, the reader is referred to the *Economic Review* for July 1961, published by the National Institute of Economic and Social Research, and to *Economic Growth in Japan and USSR* by Angus Maddison (George Allen and Unwin). These suggest that between 1870 and 1950, the total output (gnp at constant prices) grew by 264 per cent in Britain, 417 per cent in Germany, and 193 per cent in France.[1] At best, these results can only be regarded as estimates showing rankings, or orders of magnitude. But they are both interesting and illuminating.

One further point is worth mentioning at this stage. Since the war, we have become accustomed to steadily rising prices. In Britain the

---

[1] Figures for a number of other countries are quoted.

price index for consumers' goods and services rose from 61·8 in 1948 to 120·0 in 1968, an increase of 94 per cent or an annual average of 3·4 per cent. But there have been long periods in our history in which prices remained virtually stable or even declined. There was a rapid fall in prices from 1929 to 1935, and very little change between 1875 and 1913. In this case an early steep fall was offset by a long slow rise.

CHAPTER 8
PERSONAL INCOMES AND
EXPENDITURE

Introduction
In Chapter 5 we considered the gross national product as the aggregate of factor incomes. The figures showed that the largest part of these factor incomes accrued to persons in the form of wages, salaries and professional earnings. Amongst factor incomes there is, however, another important item – gross trading profits of companies. In the factor incomes approach, these profits are regarded as the income of companies, but a moment's thought will show that the major portion of the interest and dividends paid out of this company income is likely to be paid to individual shareholders. As we shall soon see, however, there are still other sources of personal incomes. It is part of our task in this chapter to examine these various sources of personal income and to analyse how the total is distributed amongst incomes of varying sizes.

In Chapter 6, the gross national product was regarded from the point of view of expenditure. Again, the largest element in total expenditure was seen to be consumers' expenditure, i.e., expenditure incurred by persons in satisfying their more immediate wants. Personal income invariably exceeds personal expenditure, consumers could not, even if they wished, spend all their earnings and income since a not inconsiderable portion is paid away as direct taxation and by way of contributions to national insurance, superannuation, and similar schemes. Even so, the average consumer still wishes to save a portion of his income. We shall see how the balance is struck between personal income and expenditure. The relevant section in the Blue Books dealing with personal income and expenditure is called, not unnaturally, the personal sector.

Categories of personal income
These can perhaps best be seen and discussed with reference to the appropriate table in the Blue Book. Table 8.1. shows the amounts received from these categories for six years from 1958 to 1968.

In the first place it will be seen that personal incomes are regarded as those incomes accruing to households (which may be of one or more individuals) and private non-profit-making bodies. The latter is of only very minor importance; examples are friendly societies and trade unions. Second, it will be seen that four main categories of personal incomes are distinguished.

(a) *Direct income in cash from work and property*

Little difficulty is likely to be met in understanding the various kinds of income included within this category. By far the largest item is wages and salaries, followed a long way behind by income from self-employment – i.e., earnings of professional people, sole traders, farmers, etc. Net income from property by way of rent, dividend, and interest in 1968 was about one tenth of that from wages and salaries and about two thirds of the income from self-employment. Pay in cash to members of the armed forces was only a minute proportion of total incomes from work and property.

(b) *Imputed income and income in kind*

This category may call for some explanation. Imputed income is a benefit received by individuals to which a value is attached, but which is not received directly or immediately in the form of cash. Rent of owner-occupied dwellings is a good example. This is the benefit which such owners are considered to receive by virtue of living in their own property; it is arrived at by estimating the rent they could expect to receive if the property were let to a tenant. It should be pointed out that a considerable proportion of owner-occupiers have to pay interest on mortgages. Such interest is clearly a deduction from income and in the national accounts it is included under 'Interest paid' in category (a), along with bank interest paid on private loans, and loans to farmers and sole traders and partnerships. Since a part of the benefits received by persons from the various social security schemes (unemployment and sickness benefits, for example) is financed from employers' contributions, these latter are properly regarded as imputed personal income. Income in kind, about one-eighth of the total of this category, is the valuation put on direct non-cash benefits such as the coal allowances paid to miners, luncheon-vouchers paid to office staff, free and reduced travel concessions to transport workers and officials, and board and lodgings provided for members of the armed forces.

Table 8.1. Categories of personal income

£ million

	1958	1960	1962	1964	1966	1968
Households and private non-profitmaking bodies						
Direct income in cash from work and property:						
Wages and salaries	11,958	13,548	15,436	17,528	20,086	22,203
Pay in cash of H.M. Forces	355	362	372	417	485	507
Income from self-employment*	1,786	2,014	2,155	2,342	2,665	2,840
Rent, dividends and interest:						
Gross receipts	1,420	1,846	2,063	2,427	2,794	3,032
less Interest paid	−254	−341	−412	−494	−670	−850
Total	15,265	17,429	19,614	22,220	25,360	27,732
Imputed income and income in kind:						
Employers' national insurance and health contributions	398	425	557	682	906	1,102
Income in kind	217	218	233	255	277	282
Rent of owner-occupied dwellings	364	418	512	643	778	933
Accrued interest on national savings certificates	−25	12	23	36	−42	−4
Total	954	1,073	1,325	1,616	1,919	2,313

£ million

	1958	1960	1962	1964	1966	1968
Current transfers to charities from companies	13	17	21	26	30	34
Current grants from public authorities:						
Retirement pensions, widows' benefits, etc., and non-contributory pensions	677	758	912	1,136	1,429	1,712
Grants to private non-profit-making bodies	730	811	973	147	205	254
Other current grants				974	1,200	1,721
Total	1,407	1,569	1,885	2,257	2,834	3,687
Pensions and other benefits from life assurance and superannuation schemes	688	778	942	1,114	1,397	1,705
Total income of households and private non-profit-making bodies, including pensions and other benefits from life assurance and superannuation schemes	18,327	20,866	23,787	27,233	31,540	35,471
Adjustment† for life assurance and superannuation funds	197	292	338	439	519	622
Total personal income	18,524	21,158	24,125	27,672	32,059	36,093

* Before providing for depreciation and stock appreciation.
† Contributions of employers *plus* rent, dividends and interest receipts *less* pensions and other benefits paid.

(c) *Current grants*

The third category of personal incomes takes the form of grants, which can be described as payments not directly or immediately related to services rendered. The largest item in this group is retirement pensions, widows' benefits and non-contributory pensions – that is, payments usually on a fixed scale from general taxation assisted perhaps by grants from national insurance funds. These are clearly forms of personal income, as are the payments coming under 'other current grants'. These are mainly unemployment, sickness, and similar benefits.

(d) *Pensions and superannuation benefits paid from wholly or mainly privately financed schemes* form the fourth category, and in volume they are about equal to the 'other current grants' in category (c). Accumulated assurance and superannuation funds are usually invested and thereby earn interest and rent. These earnings, together with employers' contributions to private schemes, amount to a general addition to the sum of the incomes detailed under the four categories distinguished above.

Trends in the total of personal income

It can be seen from table 8.1. that wages and salaries accounted for 64·6 per cent of total personal income in 1958, but only 61·5 per cent in 1968. In fact, the total contribution of direct income from work and property was a smaller proportion of total personal income in 1968 than it had been in 1958; 76·8 per cent as opposed to 82·4 per cent. Each of the three other categories increased their contribution over the ten years. A growing proportion of total personal income has therefore been coming from social security benefits and pensions, both contributory and non-contributory.

The total of personal income in relation to total factor incomes may cause some surprise. In 1958, total personal income totalled £18,524 million, and gross national product at factor cost £20,408 million. The corresponding figures in 1968 were £36,093 million and £36,686 million respectively, which means that total personal income was almost equal to gross national product. But a little thought will provide the reason for this. Some of the total for personal income is made up of transfer incomes and these are not included in the gross national product. Included in factor incomes are gross trading profits of companies; in the factor incomes analysed these are regarded as incomes to companies. In due course, however (as we have already pointed out), a large proportion of these profits are distributed as interest and dividends, and as such, form part of personal income. Thus, a very large proportion of factor incomes become part of personal income, and to this proportion transfer incomes are added.

Incomes per head of the employed population

Not very much information on this topic is obtainable solely from the Blue Books since they contain few figures of numbers employed. The major exceptions relate to wages and salaries in manufacturing industries and to the distribution of all personal incomes, by income groups, both before and after tax. From the first of these it is easy to calculate that wage earners in manufacturing industries received an average of £525 in 1958 and £923 in 1968. The corresponding figures for salary earners are £790 and £1,336. Over the same period, the estimated number of wage earners employed in manufacturing industries fell from 6·110 million to 5·685 million, whilst that of salary earners rose from 1·650 million to 2·070 million. The ten-year increase in average wages was 76 per cent; in average salaries it amounted to 70 per cent. In manufacturing industry, therefore, there was not much evidence for the widely expressed view that salaries lagged conspicuously behind wages. (This point was touched upon in Chapter 5.)

In Chapter 4, there is a section on output per head in the various sectors in which an attempt is made to associate earnings in the various sectors distinguished with employment in these sectors. The employment figures used were from various publications of the Department of Employment and Productivity. The reader may like to refer to this section in the present context of personal incomes.

Distribution of personal income before and after tax

By virtue of the income returns which the Inland Revenue require for the purpose of calculating tax liabilities, it has long been possible to draw up annual statements of personal income by income groups, both before and after the payment of direct taxation. These statements appear in the Blue Books; the one for 1969 gives these statements for 1959, 1966, and 1967. Personal income is analysed by size of income and for this purpose some 15 income groups are distinguished along with the number of incomes in each of these groups, and the total income in each before and after tax. For 1967, it was possible to allocate over £28 billion of personal income, representing

27·8 million incomes, to the 15 income ranges. Reference to table 8.1. suggests that this must be a very large part of total personal income liable for tax. In 1967 the direct income in cash from work and property was just over £26 million; pensions, and certain payments in kind are, of course, also liable for tax.

Chart 3 shows the 1959 and 1967 distribution of personal incomes in graphical form. It associates the cumulative number of incomes expressed as a percentage of the total with the cumulative amount of these incomes, also expressed as a percentage of the total. Table 8.2.

Table 8.2. Proportion of income remaining after tax, 1959 and 1967

Income range	Percentage of total income* in this range		Percentage of income* remaining after tax	
£	1959	1967	1959	1967
50–249	5·8	1·7	99·9	100·0
250–299	2·9	0·9	98·9	100·0
300–399	5·7	2·3	96·7	98·8
400–499	7·2	3·3	95·6	96·6
500–599	9·1	4·0	94·8	96·0
600–699	10·1	4·4	94·6	93·3
700–799	10·3	4·6	94·0	92·0
800–999	16·1	10·9	92·7	90·3
1,000–1,499	16·1	29·3	88·7	88·5
1,500–1,999	4·6	16·8	82·0	85·7
2,000–2,999	4·2	10·9	76·6	84·0
3,000–4,999	3·6	4·9	67·7	72·5
5,000–9,999	2·6	3·5	54·7	63·9
10,000–19,999	1·1	1·6	38·7	47·5
20,000 and over	0·6	0·8	18·2	24·5
Average			89·5	86·4

* Excluding income not classified by ranges. Total classified incomes were: 1959, £16,396 million; 1967, £28,179 million.

shows the proportion of income remaining after tax to income before tax for each of the separate income groups distinguished in the Blue Book.

As the figures appear in the Blue Book, they show the number of incomes, income before tax, and income after tax, for each of the 15 income groups separately distinguished for the years 1959 and 1967. Much useful information can be gathered from these figures about the growth of incomes over the eight years covered in the tables. Thus, in 1959, the number of incomes in the middle income ranges £700–1,500 was 7·47 million, and the income received by those in this group was £6,964 million. In 1967, the figures were 11·91 million and £12,614 million, respectively. This comparison provides a clear indication of the growing numbers coming within these middle income groups. Moreover, average income in 1959 was £618; by 1967

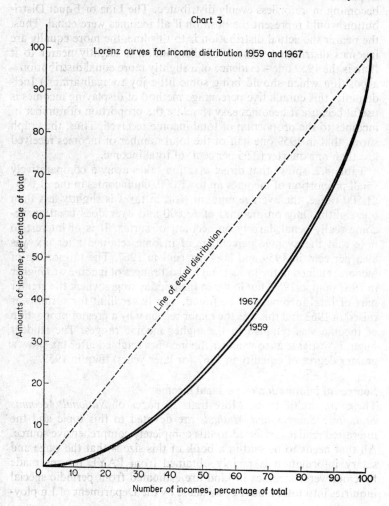

Chart 3

Lorenz curves for income distribution 1959 and 1967

this had grown to £1,014. The extent to which direct taxation – income tax and surtax – has depleted the original incomes is shown in Table 8.2.

There is a special reason for drawing up the chart of number of incomes associated with total incomes received in the way it has been done in Chart 3. This type of chart is known as a Lorenz Chart and its particular characteristic is that it shows whether or not incomes are becoming more or less evenly distributed. The Line of Equal Distribution would represent the position if all incomes were equal. Thus, the nearer the actual distribution is to this line, the more equally are incomes distributed. (The 1967 distribution is slightly nearer to it than is the 1959 one – evidence of a slightly more equal distribution – a position which should bring some little joy to egalitarians.) Incidentally, this cumulative percentage method of displaying incomes is useful because it becomes easy to relate the proportion of number of incomes to the proportion of total income received. Thus, the graph shows that in 1959 one half of the total number of incomes received less than one quarter (22·5 per cent) of total income.

Table 8.2. shows that direct taxation takes away a comparatively small proportion of incomes up to £1,000. On incomes in the £1,000–£1,500 range, the average amount paid in taxes is slightly less than one-eighth. Only on incomes of £3,000 and over does taxation become really penal, largely on account of surtax. It is of interest to note that the average percentage of income retained after tax was 89·5 per cent in 1959 and 86·4 per cent in 1967. The proportion of income retained in the lowest and highest ranges of income was higher in 1967 than in 1969, but lower in the middle ranges where the greater part of total income is to be found. The lower limit for surtax was raised in 1962 and this was the major reason why a greater proportion of income was retained in the higher income ranges. The student might investigate as to whether the incomes retained after tax show a greater degree of equality in 1967 (or later years) than in 1959.

Sources of information on personal income

These are multifarious. More than 20 pages of *National Accounts Statistics: Sources and Methods* are devoted to this topic and the interested reader is referred to this completely comprehensive source. All that needs to be said in a book of this size is that the wage and salary information is mainly obtained from PAYE returns made by employers; incomes in kind are estimated from periodic special inquiries into total labour costs made by the Department of Employment and Productivity; forces' pay is derived from the Appropriation Accounts of the Ministry of Defence; employers' contributions to national insurance and social services from Central Government Accounts; and employers' contributions to superannuation schemes from the published accounts of nationalized industries and from special studies made into privately operated schemes.

Expenditure in the personal sector

This must, of course, be governed by income in the personal sector. Income and expenditure can be regarded as the two sides of an account (in the book-keeping sense). If expenditure is less than income, the balance must be saving; if greater, the difference is borrowing. In actual practice some individuals and one-man businesses save, others borrow to cover expenditure; but on balance expenditure is less than income.

To begin with, we shall consider the main lines of expenditure in the personal sector. We have already seen that in 1968 total personal income amounted to an estimated £36,093 million. A not-inconsiderable proportion of this is immediately pre-empted by direct taxes and contributions made to national insurance and the social services generally on the part of employees and self employed persons. A small proportion of the total taxes paid are in respect of earnings from abroad. In addition, a further small item, 'Transfers abroad' – mainly migrants' remittances and gifts to overseas dependants – is regarded as having prior claims. The balance after these pre-emptions and prior claims have been met is known as 'personal disposable income' which the personal sector may spend or save. One specific form of voluntary savings made to cover future tax liabilities, known as 'additions to tax reserves', is separated out from the mass of general saving. This description can now be supplemented by the actual amounts involved.

A number of further points should be made on the items in Table 8.3. The figures for consumers' expenditure are, of course, those appearing in Chapter 6 in which gross national product is considered by category of expenditure. Saving is the balancing item between income and expenditure: it cannot be exactly verified by any one independent assessment but its validity is constantly tested by various means. To the extent that one-man businesses are included in the private sector, the savings figure can be considered as containing an unknown element for depreciation of assets and for stock appreciation. Expressed as a percentage of personal income, total savings

E

Table 8.3. Expenditure accounts of the personal sector
1958 and 1968

	£ million		
	1958		1968
Total personal income	18,524		36,093
UK taxes on income		1,696	4,559
Taxes paid abroad		11	24
Transfers abroad, net		—4	78
National insurance contributions etc.		859	2,167
Personal disposable income	15,962		29,265
Consumers' expenditure	15,296		27,065
Additions to tax reserves		50	125
Saving		616	2,075

were 3·6 per cent in 1958 and 6·1 per cent in 1968. These savings help to finance capital investment and at any given time consumers' expenditure can only be increased at the expense of savings – and therefore of capital investment.

Comparisons with income and expenditure in 1938

Total personal income for 1938 has been estimated at £5,078 million; of which income from employment was £3,022 million, or 60 per cent, and income from self-employment, £647 million, or 12 per cent. The corresponding percentages for 1968 were 70 and 8, respectively, indicating a considerable movement towards employment and away from self-employment. Another important difference lay in the share contributed by dividends and net interest. In 1938 no less than 20 per cent of personal income came from these services, compared with 12 per cent in 1968. Rents take up a much smaller proportion of personal income and expenditure than they did in pre-war days, whilst dividends have been restricted by higher taxation. These figures point to the more rapid increase in the standards of living of the so-called working classes than of other classes in society.

In 1938 consumers' expenditure, at £4,400 million, was 87 per cent of total expenditure, taxes and national health and insurance contributions, £400 million or 8 per cent, and savings, before providing for depreciation and stock appreciation, £262 million or 5·2 per cent. Compared with pre-war days, consumption in 1968 was a significantly lower proportion of total personal income, and taxation a considerably higher (18 per cent) proportion.

Categories of consumers' expenditure

Thanks to three continuing surveys, a great deal is known about the way in which consumers spend their incomes. These three surveys are: the Family Expenditure Survey carried out by the Department of Employment and Productivity, the National Food Survey of the Ministry of Agriculture and Food, and the International Passenger Survey of the Board of Trade. The main interest in the categories of personal expenditure lies in the information they provide on the spending habits of the affluent society. As the nation becomes more and more affluent, spending on food and clothing tends to fall as a percentage of total expenditure, whilst that on luxury goods and services tend to rise. This tendency is discernible over the ten years 1958 to 1968. In 1958, expenditure on food was 22·5 per cent and that on clothing, 8·5 per cent, of total spending. In 1968, the percentages were 21 and 8·33 respectively. Spending on durable goods – motor cars, furniture, radio, television, electrical goods etc. – was only 80 per cent of that on clothing in 1958. Ten years later the spending on durable goods had overtaken that on clothing. Expenditure on services (other than domestic) more than doubled over the ten years compared with a 77 per cent increase in consumers' expenditure as a whole. The spread of home ownership is indicated by expenditure on maintenance, repairs, and improvements by occupiers which increased by 140 per cent.

About 50 categories of consumers' expenditure are distinguished in the 1969 Blue Book, and expenditure at 1963 prices as well as current prices are shown. At constant prices, expenditure on food increased by 13·5 per cent and on alcoholic drink by 40 per cent, whilst it was stationary on tobacco and cigarettes. Consumers' expenditure abroad at constant prices rose fairly rapidly until 1966, after which the travel allowance limitations caused a significant decline.

The experts who compile the national income and expenditure tables have estimated the extent to which indirect taxation and subsidies figure in consumer spending. In 1968 taxes on food were more than offset by subsidies, and those on alcoholic drink increased from £399 million in 1958 to £749 million in 1968. In former years taxation accounted for 44 per cent of the price of drink paid by the consumer; this proportion had increased by less than one per cent in

1968. In the case of tobacco the percentages of taxation were 71 in 1958 and 69 in 1968. Travel was much more heavily subsidized in 1968 than in 1958. (In this case, the subsidy takes the form of making up the losses on nationalized transport.) The most heavily subsidized sector of consumer expenditure in 1968 was in rent, rates, and water charges; some £227 million. In the main, this represents housing subsidies paid to local authorities which permits them to let houses at lower than economic rents. Food subsidies amounted to £215 million in 1968, against £155 million levied as taxation on food.

The student will appreciate that the above is but a brief summary of the information provided in the Blue Books on consumers' expenditure. He should learn to regard these sources, together with the three surveys mentioned earlier, as the best indicators which we have of the levels of living standards, and of the changes in these standards.

CHAPTER 9
CAPITAL FORMATION AND
CONSUMPTION

Introduction and definitions

Capital formation means adding to the nation's stock of wealth or goods. In the national accounts, three types of capital formation are distinguished: the acquisition of fixed assets in the United Kingdom, the acquisition of stocks and work in progress, and net investment abroad. In this context, net investment abroad means the difference between investment by UK individuals and firms in other countries and the realization of foreign assets by these individuals and firms.

The acquisition of fixed assets or fixed capital formation represents additions to physical productive assets that yield a continuous service beyond the period of account (a year, in the case of the national accounts) in which they are purchased. Capital formation in stocks and work-in-progress represents additions to completed goods not yet sold, materials and fuel not yet used, and partly finished products awaiting completion. Examples of fixed capital assets are machinery, equipment, vehicles, buildings, and civil engineering works. Expenditure on durable consumer goods such as cars, washing machines, and refrigerators, which are regarded as being consumed when they are purchased, is included in consumers' expenditure although these items may last quite a long time.

When the term fixed capital formation is used it denotes gross investment in fixed assets. This means that nothing is deducted for depreciation, i.e. wear and tear, obsolescence and accidental damage. When such allowances are made the result represents the true growth in fixed assets, and the amount of the allowance can be regarded as capital consumption. This amount is by no means easy to estimate; it is in fact more hypothetical than real as we shall see later in this chapter.

Trends in gross domestic fixed capital formation and in the physical increase in stocks and work in progress

These have been discussed briefly in Chapter 6 and the relevant figures for 1958 to 1968 appear in Table 6.1. The percentage distribution of the expenditure components of gross national product for various years from 1938 to 1968 is given in Table 6.2. So far as domestic fixed capital is concerned ('domestic' implies investment in Britain only), Table 6.2. shows that over the last 20 years, investment, as a proportion of gross national product, has risen appreciably. In 1938 it was 11 per cent, in 1948 11·75 per cent, but by 1968 it had risen to 18 per cent. Expressed in current prices, gross domestic fixed capital formation was £3,500 million in 1958 and £7,800 million in 1968. This increase is equivalent to an average annual growth of 8 per cent at current, and 6 per cent at constant prices.

However, in Britain as in most industrial countries, growth in fixed capital formation tends to be somewhat erratic. If the business outlook is good then industry is usually more willing to invest than when the outlook is poor. Moreover, the government may take steps to check investment if the economy is in danger of overloading and encourage it when the government decides that the economy needs a stimulus. Investment may be slowed down by making it dearer for businesses to borrow money and by withdrawing or reducing investment incentives such as investment grants and allowances. Conversely, if investment is to be stimulated, loans are made easier and grants and allowances increased. The public sector may also speed up or slow down its own rate of investment.

At constant prices, the year-on-year growth in fixed investment from 1958 to 1968 was 7·7 per cent, 9·8 per cent, 9·7 per cent, 1·8 per cent, 16·3 per cent, 4·0 per cent, 2·6 per cent, 6·9 per cent, and 4·1 per cent. The year in which investment growth fell to 1·8 per cent was 1962 when the government of the day made a determined effort to check inflation in order to bring the balance of payments into surplus. In the next year, all controls on investment were removed, a stimulus was given to higher consumer spending by reducing purchase tax and easing hire purchase restrictions. The public sector was encouraged to invest more, particularly in the Development Areas. Hence the extremely high rate of growth which, of itself, added between 2·5 and 3 per cent to gross national product. Gross fixed investment is therefore a rather volatile element in the economy and one that lends itself to manipulation by the central authority.

Another volatile element in the national accounts is stockbuilding or, as it appears in the accounts, 'Value of physical (i.e. real) increase in stocks and work in progress'. This must be regarded as capital investment since it adds to the nation's stock of goods. In total, it is a comparatively small element but its fluctuations may affect the gross

national product by as much as 1·5 per cent. Table 6·1 shows its variations over the decade 1958 to 1968. Stocks and work in progress tend
to rise rapidly in the early stages of a spurt in output and to rise only a
little when the spurt or boom is over. Production can only be increased fairly rapidly when adequate stocks of raw materials are
available and there is a growing volume of work-in-progress in hand.
Hence, there was a rapid build up of stocks in 1960 and 1964, with a
relative run-down in 1962 and 1966 and 1967. After the spurt has
passed its peak, demand tends more and more to be met by turning as
much work-in-progress as possible into completed goods and selling
these without replacing all the rundown work-in-progress. It is possible, also, that financial stringency represented by high interest
rates may discourage businesses from holding large stocks.

Gross fixed investment
We shall now turn to a more systematic study of gross fixed investment, by considering it from the points of view of the sectors under-
taking it, the types of investment undertaken and the share of
industrial investment undertaken by the main industrial groups.

Distribution of investment among the various sectors of the economy
In the national income and expenditure accounts it is usual to
distinguish five main sectors of the economy: the personal sector,
companies, public corporations, central government, and local
authorities. It is hardly necessary to define 'sector' in this context
except to say that the five groups include readily identifiable types
of economic organizations. For some purposes, it is convenient to
group the first two together as the private sector and the remaining
three as the public sector. This is a further grouping by type of ownership.

One of the tables in the 1969 Blue Book gives a detailed tabulation
of the investment undertaken by each of these five main groups for
the period 1958 to 1968 and also distinguishes the kind of investment
undertaken. In the table which follows only the total fixed investment
for 1958 and 1968 is shown for these sectors

We have already seen that the personal sector includes one-man
businesses and partnerships; companies are, of course, incorporated
companies, and public corporations are, broadly speaking, the nationalized industries and organizations. They occupy a position
somewhere between direct government trading undertakings and
private enterprises. Examples of nationalized industries are British

Table 9.1. Gross domestic fixed capital formation by sector

| | £ million, 1958 prices | |
	1958	1968
Personal sector	552	1,132
Companies	1,457	2,849
Public corporations	694	1,639
Central government		
Trading	139	42
Non-trading	106	414
Local authorities		
Trading	304	921
Non-trading	240	801
Total	3,492	7,798*

* At constant 1963 prices, the figures are £3,737 million and £6,791 million, respectively.

Railways, the National Coal Board, and the British Steel Corporation.[1] The BBC, the Post Office, and the British Airports Authority are examples of nationalized organizations, although the difference between an industry and an organization is not very clearly drawn and not of great significance.

Central government trading bodies. Quite a number of government departments directly control manufacturing and trading establishments. Thus, the Ministry of Defence owns a large number of Royal Ordnance Factories, whilst the Ministry of Technology is directly responsible for a number of research and development establishments.[2] The Royal Mint is a department of the Treasury. Non-trading bodies which undertake a great deal of investment are those ministries responsible for building and equipping hospitals, universities, trunk roads, government offices, etc.

Local authorities carry on many trading activities – local transport, markets, water-works, docks and harbours, for example. Amongst the important non-trading activities are the construction of houses, schools, roads, and engineering works. Some of these activities are, however, partly or wholly financed by the central government.

---

[1] See also Chapter 5. page 27.
[2] This responsibility is now shared between the Department of Trade and Industry and the Ministry of Aviation Supply.

The immediate impression gained from the figures in Table 9.1. is that the emphasis has tended to move from the private to the public sector. As regards public corporations, the increase partly arises from the renationalization of the iron and steel and transport industries. The trading activities of the central government have declined progressively since the end of the war but in recent years those of local authorities have resulted in a rapid increase in investment. Even so, investment in non-trading activities of the central government and local authorities has risen faster than trading activities. It is a matter of argument whether social capital – hospitals, houses, roads, schools, etc. – is more productive of economic growth than industrial capital. In the short run, it is probably less productive. The growing proportion of the national investment being undertaken by the public sector implies a greater control by the state over the level of investment and the greater possibility of directing it into specific purposes and industries. Moreover, the central government can more easily manipulate the level of investment in its attempt to control economic growth.

Types of investment
The 1969 Blue Book distinguishes nine different types of investment. In this context, the word 'type' relates both to the use to which the investment is put, and to the user of the investment. Table 9.2. gives the figures for 1958 and 1968.

Table 9.2. Gross fixed capital formation (current prices) by type of asset

	£ million	
	1958	1968
Buses and coaches	18	30
Other road vehicles	232	475
Railway rolling stock	85	30
Ships	159	235
Aircraft	36	83
Plant and machinery	1,328	2,922
Dwellings	586	1,585
Other new buildings and works	1,004	2,372
Transfer costs of land and buildings	44	66
Total	3,492	7,798

The first five of these types are bought by transport undertakings or by commercial and industrial firms to move their own goods. An efficient transport system is essential for economic growth. At first sight it is a little disturbing to find that expenditure on transport equipment increased by less than the national average of all investment between 1958 and 1968. It is true, of course, that railway rolling stock, ships and aircraft are assets with a fairly long life which do not, therefore, require to be replaced at frequent intervals. But 'other road vehicles' usually have a short life. The fall in the expenditure on railway rolling stock can be ascribed to the completion of the massive railway reorganization whereby steam locomotives have been replaced by diesel and electric ones.

Plant and machinery must be regarded as the main aid to industrial growth and efficiency. It accounted for 38 per cent of total investment in 1958, and 37·5 per cent in 1968. Other new buildings and works comprise both industrial and social capital – new factories, offices, roads and bridges, as well as new schools and hospitals. It is impossible to say how much is industrial and commercial, and how much is social. Dwellings must be regarded as social capital although they have, no doubt, some effect on industrial efficiency. Their share of total investment rose from 17 per cent to over 20 per cent. The final item, transfer costs, represents legal charges and stamp duty on transfers of land and buildings. This is regarded as adding to the value of the asset and hence as capital investment.

Gross fixed capital formation by industry
A very useful table allocates gross fixed investment by major types – vehicles, ships, aircraft; plant and machinery; new buildings and works – and total investment to eleven major industrial and service groups. Thus, it is possible to say that manufacturing industry invested £922 million in 1958 and £1,565 million in 1968, and the distributive trades £203 million and £387 million in these two years. In view of the total rise in investment over the ten years, the rise in that undertaken by manufacturing industry seems disappointingly small. However, the industries producing gas, water and electricity (supplying both consumers and industrialists) showed a 133 per cent increase in investment. Investment in the so-called social and other public services rose from £327 million in 1958 to £1,190 million in 1968, an increase of over 260 per cent. When this is added to the investment in dwellings, i.e., the cost of new houses and major reconstructions of existing dwellings, the conclusion that an unduly large proportion of total investment is finding its way to social, rather than industrial and commercial ends, can hardly be avoided.

Capital consumption and capital stock

At the same time as the public and private sectors are spending money on capital investment, the existing stock of capital is being eroded. Wear and tear, fire, and similar damage and obsolescence are all taking their toll. The reduction in capital assets through these causes is known as capital consumption or depreciation, although the latter term should strictly be applied to wear and tear only. The loss of assets through fire and similar damage can be assessed fairly accurately, as also can that due to obsolescence – i.e. replacing existing assets not only because they are worn out but because they have become out of date. Depreciation cannot be measured directly since it is the service provided by fixed assets which is being used up; the assets themselves are not being consumed. Its estimation, as we have already pointed out, is fraught with difficulties and involves a judgement of the length of time that the asset will be giving service. Businesses provide for depreciation in their accounts but these provisions are not suitable for the national accounts. For one thing they are usually based on original cost of the asset and take no account of the increases in price since purchase. For another, they are not necessarily calculated on a consistent basis between different firms. The compilers of the national accounts are therefore thrown back on their own resources, as it were, in estimating capital consumption.

The method used in estimating capital stock and capital consumption is known as the perpetual inventory method.[1] Suffice it to say here that gross capital stock and capital consumption by sector industry and by type of asset, have been estimated for every year from 1948 to the present time. Thus, the gross capital stock at 1963 replacement cost was estimated at £70,700 million in 1948, £89,700 million in 1958, and £127,600 million in 1968. In 1958, capital consumption was estimated at £1,903 million (1963 prices). Thus capital consumption in 1958 represented 2·1 per cent of gross capital stock. In 1968, the proportion was 2·3 per cent.

Naturally, capital consumption is at a slower rate in the case of assets with a long life than with those having a short one. Thus in 1968 the stock of dwellings was estimated to be worth £38,000 million; and capital consumption was given as £443 million,[2] or only a

---

[1] For information on this method, see the appropriate references in the Bibliography at the end of this book.
[2] At 1963 prices.

little over one per cent. The corresponding figures for plant and machinery were: stock, £16,960 million;[1] capital consumption, £1,347 million.[1] In this case capital consumption was nearly 8 per cent of capital stock.

The difference between gross capital formation and capital consumption is known as net domestic fixed capital formation. This represents the addition, year by year, to the net capital stock. The latter, being the difference between gross capital stock and capital consumption, can be thought of as the best estimate which can be made of the real national capital. At current replacement cost, this is estimated at £48,000 million in 1958 and £93,000 million in 1968. In 1958 net domestic fixed capital formation was some 3·5 per cent of net capital stock; by 1968 the proportion had risen to just under 5 per cent. This increase must give some cause for satisfaction, but this is tempered somewhat if the comparison is related to vehicles, plant and machinery only. The percentage increase was much the same in the two years, rather less than 5 per cent.

It will be recalled that the difference between gross national product and gross national income is identical with capital consumption. This latter represented 8·8 per cent of gross national product in 1958 and 9·2 per cent in 1968. As a percentage of gross capital formation it is of course very much higher, about 50 per cent in 1958 and 45 per cent ten years later.

The financing of investment

As we saw in Chapter 6, investment is only one of three major competing claims on the gross national product – personal consumption and public expenditure on goods and services being the other two. Investment can only be undertaken if and when there are resources left over when public and private consumption spending have had their share. This means that both the public and private sector must save some of their income. In the last chapter, a balance was drawn up between income and expenditure in the personal sector and it was seen that in 1968, £2,200 million was available for investment. Similar statements can be drawn up for each of the other four sectors but the aggregation of the surpluses is complicated by the fact that there are transfers between sectors. Perhaps we can best begin our study of the financing of investment by looking at the capital account for the country as a whole.

---

[1] At 1963 prices.

Table 9.3. Savings and investment – all sectors, 1968 (£ million)

	Saving	Gross domestic fixed capital formation	Increase in stocks and work in progress	Net investment abroad
Personal sector	2,200	1,132	192	
Industrial and commercial companies	3,044	2,494	604	
Financial institutions	260	355	–	
Public Sector	3,012	3,817	58	
Overseas	–	–	–	
Total	8,516	7,798	854	—265

This table shows that the total saving by all sectors amounted to
£8,516 million in 1968. This was matched by £7,798 million gross
domestic fixed capital formation, £854 million increase in stocks and
work-in-progress, and —£265 million net investment abroad. These
three types of investment were distinguished in the first paragraph of
this chapter. Together they added up to £8,387 million, or £129 million less than the total savings of the nation. This £129 million is the
same figure as the residual error shown in the matching up of gross
national product obtained by the factor incomes and the industry and
service origin methods. When this residual error is allowed for, the
Keynesian identity of savings and investment is reached.

The capital transfers between sectors have been omitted from Table
9.3. They do, of course, balance out but the Blue Book table from
which the details in Table 9.3. were taken shows that industrial and
commercial companies received £431 million from this source which
was offset by outgoings of £230 million in the personal sector, £11
million in insurance companies etc. and £190 million in the public
sector.

Savings in the non-personal sectors

Industrial and commercial companies
Savings in this sector arise when company income obtained from
trading profits and non-trading income (interest and rent, for example) are not wholly paid out by way of taxes on company income
and dividends and interest paid to shareholders. In 1968, total company income amounted to an estimated figure of £8,559 million. From

this sum, £3,108 million was paid out as dividends and interest in the United Kingdom and £319 million abroad; taxation on income in the UK and overseas took £1,794 million, and £34 million represented transfers to charities. This leaves £3,044 million, the total of savings shown in Table 9.3. Clearly, the more profit made by industrial and commercial concerns, the greater the potential sum available for savings and investment. This potential sum is reduced by dividend and interest paid to shareholders and debenture holders. It is also reduced by taxation on company income, a fair proportion of which is paid to foreign governments.

If the industrial and commercial companies are lumped with financial institutions in Table 9.3., it will be seen that their total saving is £3,304 million and their total investment is £3,453 million. Reference to the appropriate account of companies, however, shows that in addition to this investment, companies paid £17 million in taxes on capital and their financial assets including investment abroad rose by £271 million. Financial assets represent savings held in the form of cash in banks, shares in other companies and investment abroad. The total investment of these companies therefore amounted to £3,741 million. The difference between this sum and their sector savings – *viz.*, £437 million – came from capital transfers, mainly in the form of 'investment grants' (£410 million).

Investment grants first appeared in the national accounts for 1967. They are grants paid by the central government to encourage investment by industry and to direct some of this investment to the development areas. Prior to 1967, investment incentives took the form of allowing firms to write off, out of profits, a large proportion of their capital investment in the year in which it was undertaken. This, by reducing their book profits, reduced the tax they were required to pay on their profits for the year in question. But this concession was only a deferment, not a real reduction. Large sums are now being paid by the government on investment grants but these have not noticeably increased the volume of investment, which seems to be related more to total consumer demand and the general economic outlook.[1]

Public corporations
Table 9.1. shows that the gross fixed investment of public corporations was £1,639 million in 1968. To this must be added an increase of £23

---

[1] The present Government (1971) has returned to the investment allowance system.

million in stocks and work-in-progress and a £328 million net acquisition of financial assets. Net income of public corporations in 1968 only slightly exceeded £800 million, to which must be added £100 million by way of capital transfers. These figures imply an investment in excess of savings of about £1,100 million. This difference is shown in the relevant Blue Book table to have been made up by loans from the central government. These have long been a feature of the capital accounts of the public corporations; they were £576 million in 1958. Generally speaking, the public corporations themselves finance less than half their total investment.

Central government
Table 9.1. shows that gross fixed capital formation by the central government was £456 million in 1968; increase in the value of stocks added a further £35 million to this. However, no less than £3,137 million was paid out on capital account; £850 million of this was in capital transfers, £415 million in investment grants to the private sector, and £35 million to public corporations. The remainder was spent on capital grants to local authorities, universities and similar bodies. In addition, £1,757 million went out in loans to local authorities, public corporations, overseas governments and industry.

The central government current account had a surplus of £1,750 million, and £439 million of this came from taxes on capital. The largest element in this latter was death duties (£374 million) and capital gains tax (£53 million). About £200 million was derived from a miscellany of sources, leaving a balance of over £750 million to be covered by borrowing. Some of this was lent by the Bank of England (over £300 million, in fact), about £100 million by overseas governments, and most of the remainder by the International Monetary Fund. In 1968, Britain had a very large deficit on its balance of payments and recourse had to be made to loans to cover this deficit whilst keeping the gold and currency reserves at a more or less constant level. These loans are regarded as being on capital account. A not-insignificant part of Britain's investment in 1968 was therefore financed by foreign governments and international concerns.

Local authorities
These invested £1,722 million in 1968 and in addition made small capital grants of £23 million to the private sector; the surplus of their current accounts was £446 million, leaving about £1,300 million uncovered. Current grants from the central government provided £144

million, borrowing from the central government, £589 million, and other borrowing, £566 million.

Transfers from the personal sector to other sectors
It is clear from Table 9.3. that only the personal sector has a balance of savings over investment – £876 million in 1968. This is available for lending to industry either directly, by taking up new shares and debentures, or through banks and insurance companies (i.e., institutional lending and investment), and for lending to the government and local authorities. However, lending to the government on the part of the personal sector in the form of national savings, which exceeded £209 million in 1964, has since then become negative, since withdrawals have exceeded new lending. This process was reversed in 1970 however.

CHAPTER 10
INCOME AND EXPENDITURE IN
THE PUBLIC SECTOR

Introduction and scope of the Study

In the immediately preceding chapter, we considered that part of public expenditure which is devoted to capital investment, and we looked at this investment in the context of national investment as a whole. In the present chapter we shall be extending the study of public expenditure to take in current, that is, non-capital expenditure of the central government and local authorities. We have already discussed, very briefly, the category of expenditure known as public authorities' current expenditure on goods and services (Chapter 6). This was shown to be £7,702 million in 1968, but the addition of the current expenditure of the central government and local authorities gives a figure of about £18,500 million (including current surpluses).

This latter figure, however, contains a significant element of transfer payments between the central government and local authorities, particularly in regard to education and housing, and the central government current expenditure also contains a very large element of other transfer payments – subsidies, grants, debt interest, and social security benefits. These have no counterpart in the output of goods and services, and they appear as incomes in the other sectors or as elements of gross national product at market prices. On the incomes side a cursory examination will be made of the main sources of income of both central government and local authorities. Finally, we shall make a reference to what has become known as the Treasury analysis of public expenditure. This covers the entire net expenditure of central and local government, but sets it down in accordance with a functional classification.

Central government income and expenditure on current account 1958 and 1968

(a) *Income*. Table 10.1. sets out the income of the central government under a number of summary headings. Following this, a brief analysis on the elements making up the headings is given.

Table 10.1. Income of central government on current account, 1958 and 1968

		£ million	
		1958	*1968*
(i)	Taxes on income	2,725	5,649
(ii)	Taxes on expenditure	2,192	4,242
(iii)	Taxes and levies, mainly on industry and services	198	1,150
(iv)	National health and insurance contributions	859	2,167
(v)	Rent, interest and dividends, including trading surpluses	464	984
	Total	6,438	14,192

* In 1958, this also includes £3 million – defence aid from the USA

(i) *Taxes on income*
These include income tax together with surtax, profits tax and, from 1966, corporation tax, which is taking the place of profits tax. Over the decade, income tax increased from £2,285 million to £4,168 million. In 1958, it produced five-sixths of the total taxes on income, but with the growth of corporation tax from £23 million in 1966 to £1,249 million in 1968, its share declined to less than three-quarters in 1968. Surtax yielded £161 million in 1958. This rose to £230 million in 1962 but with the raising of the limit at which surtax becomes payable, there was some decline in the next few years. By 1968 the yield had, however, recovered to £220 million. Profits tax rose from £276 million in 1958 to £465 million in 1965, but declined steeply thereafter to yield only £12 million in 1968. Taxes on income are, of course, examples of direct taxation, and the claim is often made that high rates of direct taxation are inimical to effort and therefore to business efficiency. In relation to taxes on expenditure, the yield on direct taxation has grown the faster, but if profits tax and corporation tax are omitted, the growth of taxation on personal incomes has been slower.

(ii) *Taxes on expenditure*
In total, the yield of these taxes grew by 94 per cent between 1958 and 1968. The five main sources of revenue – tobacco, purchase tax, hydrocarbon oils, beer, wines and spirits – produced just over 90 per cent of the total in 1958 and just over 92 per cent in 1968 but their

individual growths have differed considerably as successive Parliaments have raised the rates of tax. In 1958, the tax on tobacco yielded £734 million; this had increased to £1,083 million by 1968. The yield of the duty on hydrocarbon oils (motor fuel) more than trebled from £341 million to £1,081 million – making it equal to that on tobacco. Its growth was much more rapid after 1964 than from 1958 to 1964. This also applies to purchase tax which produced £497 million in 1958 and £971 million in 1968. The tax on alcoholic drink rose from £414 million to £775 million over the same period, but the yield on wines and spirits which was only three-fifths of that on beer in 1968 had become practically equal to it in 1968.

Of the remaining taxes on expenditure, protective duties (taxes on imports) rose fairly steadily from £110 million in 1958 to £183 million in 1964. Thereafter their growth was much more hesitant, due probably to the effect of the 'Kennedy Round' of tariff reductions. The 1968 yield was £224 million. The temporary surcharge on imports enacted in late 1964 produced £26 million in that year, and £300 million in 1965 and 1966 taken together, after which it was abolished. Betting taxation remained fairly constant from 1958 to 1966, yielding about £35 million a year; higher rates brought up the yield to £97 million in 1968.

(iii) *Taxes and levies mainly on industries and services*
As Table 10.1. shows these produced nearly six times as much in 1968 as in 1958, largely due to the imposition of selective employment tax in 1966. This produced £299 million in 1966, £434 million in 1967, and £619 million in 1968. About one third of this is returned as employment premiums to manufacturing firms. The other main tax in this group is motor vehicle licence duties, the yield of which rose from £106 million in 1958 to £194 million in 1964. Thereafter the increase was rapid to £385 million in 1968.

(iv) *Contributions*
Much the same story is repeated in the case of national health and insurance contributions which rose from £859 million in 1958 to £1,444 million in 1964 and to £2,067 million in 1968. The latter figure includes a smallish new element—redundancy fund contributions.

Items (i) to (iv) are receipts from taxation. Item (v) represents income from services rendered, largely returns on money lent to local authorities and public corporations. The advent of the Labour government in 1964 marks a turning point in taxation rates and taxation revenue. Between 1958 and 1964, tax receipts from items (i) to (iv) rose by an average of 5·8 per cent a year: between 1964 and 1968 the rise averaged 11·2 per cent.

Central government expenditure on current account 1958 and 1968
As in the previous section, we shall deal with this under main headings. The relevant table in the 1969 Blue Book distinguishes at least 40 headings against which expenditure occurs; this is rather too detailed for our purpose. Table 10.2 shows this expenditure for 1958 and 1968.

Table 10.2. Central government: current expenditure 1958 and 1968

	£ million		
	1958	1968	1968 as percentage of 1958
(i) Current expenditure on goods and services	2,569	4,761	185
(ii) Subsidies	356	801	225
(iii) Current grants to personal sector	1,374	3,554	234
(iv) Miscellaneous grants and debt interest	1,517	3,326	219
(v) Total expenditure	5,816	12,442	214
(vi) Balance: current surplus*	622	1,750	281
(v) + (vi) = Total income	6,438	14,192	220

* Before providing for depreciation and stock appreciation.

Trends 1958–1968. These necessarily follow fairly closely the trends found to exist in current income since income = expenditure plus current surplus and the surplus is a relatively small part of total expenditure, albeit a somewhat volatile one. Between 1958 and 1964, expenditure grew by an annual average of 6·5 per cent; this compares with an average of 11 per cent for 1964–1968.

Within these overall growth rates, the largest rate of increase in expenditure occurred in current grants to the personal sector, and the least in current expenditure on goods and services. But the growth range is not very large.

(i) *Current expenditure on goods and services*
This is the central government portion of public authorities' current expenditure on goods and services first discussed in Chapter 6. It is

made up of one large item, military defence, which accounts for about half the total; one moderately large one, the national health service, about one quarter of the total; and a large number of small items. The current expenditure on military defence rose steadily from £1,466 million in 1958 to £2,368 in 1968, that on the national health service from £632 million to £1,373 million. In this case there appears to have been a quickening in the rate of growth in the more recent years. In both cases, there is an element of expenditure in the central government capital account. In the current account the expenditure on wages, salaries, supplies and general running expenses is recorded. There are 15 other headings in this group, which again relate to wages, salaries, supplies and running expenses; classified partly by function and partly by the government department responsible for the expenditure. Thus, finance and tax collection – £86 million to £183 million – is the cost of the Treasury inland revenue and customs and excise departments; external relations – £49 million to £106 million – is the cost of the Foreign and Commonwealth Offices (now amalgamated).

(ii) *Subsidies*
The groups (ii), (iii), and (iv) above are all transfer or equivalent headings, the payments are not made in return for services rendered. Hence they do not appear in the gross national product at factor cost. Subsidies are payments made to other sectors for the purpose of retrieving a loss made on services to the public, or a reduction of profit incurred by selling products to the public at an artificially low figure. They are, as we have seen, part of the adjustment necessary to convert gross national product at market prices to gross national product at factor cost.

The largest item is agriculture and food. In total, the agriculture and food subsidies did not vary much over the ten years, and despite fluctuations, the 1968 total was £258 million compared with £266 million in 1958. Employment premiums began in 1967 with, as we have already seen, payments of £152 million rising to £191 million in 1968. All forms of industrial and commercial enterprises pay selective employment tax (SET) based on the numbers of their employees. Enterprises engaged in manufacture have their premiums returned, together with a bonus, for being engaged in manufacture and not in merchanting or service trades. Part of the losses made by nationalized transport undertakings on their general services have been made good by the central government; this can be regarded as a subsidy paid to reimburse British Rail for carrying goods and passengers at uneconomic rates. These particular subsidies began in 1960 at £115 million; by 1968 they had risen to £151 million. Housing subsidies are paid to local authorities in order to enable them to let council houses at uneconomic rents. These rose from £81 million in 1958 to £142 million in 1968.

(iii) *Current grants to the personal sector*

As we have seen, these are the most rapidly growing items, the largest of which, social security benefits, rose from £1,272 million to £3,174 million. They cover retirement pensions, national insurance benefits, supplementary (assistance) benefits and family allowances. Of the remaining items, education grants (grants to universities, colleges, etc.; scholarships and maintenance allowances, etc.) are the most important, rising from £57 million to £228 million. These grants are paid direct to the recipients; the main grants for education occur in the next group.

(iv) *Miscellaneous grants and debt interest*

Interest paid on the national debt in all its forms rose from £780 million in 1958 to £1,249 million in 1968, due mainly to higher interest rates. During the same period current grants to local authorities rose from £660 million to £1,899 million. With the introduction of the 'Block Grant' system in 1959, the bulk of these grants are not allocated to specific services. Their use is at the option of the receiving authority, but legal requirements and official recommendations enormously limit this 'option'. The third largest item in this group is current grants to overseas countries and international organizations. This rose from £69 million in 1958 to £155 million in 1968. In the main, this comprises grant aid given to the under-developed and developing countries. Its recent low level has been the subject of controversy but deficits on the balance of payments have restricted its growth.

(vi) *Balance or surplus of income over expenditure*

As forced savings, this balance is properly regarded as income on capital account.[1] In pre-Keynesian days, the aim of Chancellors of the Exchequer was to attain a small surplus – this was regarded as good budgeting. Nowadays, the size of the current surplus is a factor in fighting inflation, or in assisting reflation.

---

[1] See Chapter 9.

Over the ten years covered by Table 10.2. the balance has varied from £202 million to the £1,750 million achieved in 1968. The average for the four years 1965–1968 was £1,225 million; for the previous six years, the average was £430 million. When steps are being taken to hold back consumers' demand, the achievement of a large surplus on current account can be an effective means to this end for it removes its own volume of consumer purchasing power. It has been so used in the years 1958, 1962, and from 1965–1968. Years in which it has been deemed desirable to reflate demand – 1960 and 1963, in particular – have been years of modest surpluses, less than £250 million, in fact. Were reflation on a large scale thought to be necessary, a 'Budget deficit' might well be one of the methods adopted.

Local authorities' income and expenditure on current account

Income

There are three main sources of local authority income: current grants from the central government, local rates, and income from trading and service activities, rent, interest, and gross trading surpluses.

As we have just noted, the bulk of current grants from the central government are not allocated to specific services, those for the police and roads and public lighting are the chief exceptions. Table 10.3. outlines the main sources of total income in 1958 and 1968.

Table 10.3. Income of local authorities on current account

	£ million	
	1958	1968
(i) Current grants:		
Not allocated to specific services	114	1,706
Specific grants	546	193
(ii) Rates	650	1,568
(iii) Gross trading surplus*	42	81
(iv) Rent and interest		
Dwellings	198	504
Other land and buildings	76	238
Interest	28	93
Total	1,654	4,383

* Before providing for depreciation and stock appreciation.

1959 was the first year in which the 'Block Grant' system operated and over the next nine years this grant increased from £410 million to £1,706 million. Rate receipts increased steadily up to 1964, more sharply afterwards. Rents of dwellings have increased fairly regularly on account of both higher rents and a growing volume of local authority-owned houses. In 1958, current grants accounted for 40 per cent of local authority income, by 1968 the proportion had risen to 44 per cent. The gross trading surplus represents the net income from trading activities, transport undertakings, markets, etc.

Expenditure
This divides into three main classes, current expenditure on goods and services, interest paid on loans, and current grants or subsidies paid to the personal sector. Current expenditure on goods and services in 1968 was £2,941 million, which, together with the same category of expenditure by the central government (£4,761 million), constitutes the item 'Public authorities' current expenditure on goods and services (£7,702 million) in Table 6.1.

Table 10.4 illustrates these classes of expenditure.

Table 10.4. Expenditure of local authorities on current account

		£ million	
		1958	*1968*
(i)	Current expenditure on goods and services	1,181	2,941
(ii)	Interest paid on loans	241	778
(iii)	(a) Housing subsidies	29	85
	(b) Current grants	33	133
	Total expenditure	1,484	3,937
(iv)	Balance – current surplus	170	446
	Total	1,654	4,383

Item (i) includes most of the activities of local authorities; the cost of many services is shared between the local authorities and the central government, the latter providing grants to cover a part, perhaps a large part, of the expenditure actually incurred by the local authorities. Education and the police force are cases in point. The social services – education, national health service, local welfare services and child care, school meals and milk – is the largest single category of expenditure. This category accounted for £715 million in 1958 and £1,823 million ten years later. As percentages of the total of expenditure on goods and services, the figures represent 61 and 62 per cent, respectively. Education is by far the largest item in this category, with expenditure on it rising from £548 million in 1958 to £1,424 million in 1968.

Other important items (from the angle of cost) are the police force, roads, and environmental services (sewerage and refuse disposal, public health services, parks and pleasure grounds, etc.).

(ii) Since capital expenditure on the part of local authorities is not usually financed out of the rates (except to the extent that the balance on current account is transferred to capital account), the finance must come from loans made by the central government and the personal sector. The interest paid on these loans is charged to the current account and, as Table 10.4. shows, it is a considerable amount. In 1958, the interest paid was distributed more or less equally between government loans and others; in 1968, the government proportion had fallen to less than one third.

(iii) Housing subsidies are the local authorities' contribution to this item, and under current grants come scholarships and grants to universities and colleges, etc.

(iv) Balance. This is transferred to the income side of the capital account of local authorities: it is another form of 'forced savings', rates income being in excess of expenditure. The total 'forced savings' arising from central and local government activities rose from £792 million in 1958 to £2,196 million in 1968. This latter amount is equivalent to 27 per cent of the savings required to finance total investment in 1968.

Treasury analysis of public expenditure
Within recent years, a special table under this heading has appeared in the annual Blue Books. Its purpose is to provide an analysis of total public expenditure which will measure expenditure against specified public expenditure programmes. This table is based on fiscal years, 1 April to 31 March, but the figures are consistent with those in calendar years which have been discussed earlier in this chapter and in the public sector discussions of Chapter 9.

We have already seen that a division of expenditure into capital and current expenditure cuts right across a number of categories; expenditure on education, defence and the social services, for example, is to be found in both capital and current accounts. Expenditure on education and some of the social services appears in both central government and local authority accounts. In education and the maintenance of law and order the responsibility for most of the expenditure lies with local authorities, but the central government makes very large grants towards such expenditure. The Treasury analysis sets out the total public expenditure, net of duplication or transfers, under some 20 or more main headings and about 100 sub-headings for the last ten fiscal years. The total of this expenditure has risen from £9,017 million in 1959/60 to £19,169 million in 1968/69. These figures include both debt interest and the capital investment of the nationalized industries.

The implications of these total figures should not be overlooked. Including the payment of debt interest and the capital expenditure of the nationalized industries, just over one half of the gross national product in 1968/69 can be considered as coming within the sphere of the public sector. Ten years earlier, the proportion was 45 per cent. Those who favour an extension of the scope of government activity will applaud this rise; those who do not will deplore it. A great deal of this expenditure finds its way back to the individual in cash or in services. But it is paid for largely by taxation. The individual might prefer to have a greater control over his own income than is possible with public expenditure so high.

In addition to the totals, a number of sub-totals attract a great deal of attention. Social security cost over £3,300 million in 1968/69, education and local libraries and museums, £2,300 million, and defence just over £2,400 million. (In 1969/70, education expenditure may well have exceeded that on defence.) Health and welfare cost £1,770 million and public sector housing, £1,100 million.

Little is said in the Blue Book about public expenditure at constant prices – at least so far as the Treasury analysis is concerned. It is true that the tables of expenditure and output at 1963 prices give figures for public authorities' current expenditure on goods and services, and divide the total into four parts – military defence, national health service, education, and other. Fixed capital formation in the public sector is also expressed at constant 1963 prices. There is, however, an element of artificiality in expressing current expenditure, which is made up to a large degree by wages, salaries and forces' pay, at constant prices. This process removes one of the main inflationary factors in public expenditure. It is all very well to say that military defence, at constant prices, is decreasing. But if it is increasing at current prices and the increase is due solely to higher forces' pay, without, as one would suspect, any improvement in defence capability, defence is costing more, not less. This difficulty highlights one weakness in assessing gross national expenditure at constant prices. No doubt the compilers of the analysis of public expenditure are acutely aware of this.

Part 3 Application of National Income Accounting

CHAPTER 11
THE USE OF NATIONAL INCOME AND EXPENDITURE ACCOUNTS IN ECONOMIC FORECASTING AND ECONOMIC MANAGEMENT

Introduction

In most of the preceding chapters we have studied the national income and expenditure tables on account of the light they can throw upon various aspects of the British economy. For this purpose we have used annual figures relating to earlier years up to and including 1968. But for a more up-to-date assessment of the country's economic position it becomes necessary to use quarterly estimates. These have been produced for a number of years now by the Central Statistical Office and they appear in *Economic Trends* and the *Monthly Digest of Statistics*. These quarterly estimates cover the summary gnp tables and, where relevant, the figures are given at both current and constant prices. Again, where relevant, the results are given on a seasonally adjusted basis in addition to the actual figures.

Seasonal adjustments are important where definite seasonal patterns of income and expenditure occur. For example, the amount of overtime worked in industry, and income from employment, vary from quarter to quarter; payment of direct taxation other than PAYE is heavily concentrated in the first quarter of the year; consumers' expenditure is usually at a peak in the few weeks before Christmas with a lesser peak in the holiday season. Seasonal adjustments remove the effect of these regular variations and reveal the underlying trend in any series.

These quarterly estimates are available about one-quarter in arrear. That is to say, the fourth quarter 1969 estimates, together with estimates for the whole year, can be expected, and were in fact published, around the beginning of the second quarter of 1970. Economists, particularly those in government service, need to produce quarterly estimates of gross national product for about a year ahead. When the Chancellor is planning his Budget he will wish to know how the economy is likely to move in the forthcoming financial year. Both his expected revenue from taxation and his plans for guiding the economy will depend upon these forward estimates. Industrial and commercial concerns, too, usually wish to have the latest quarterly gross national product figures and estimates for the next 12 months in order to do their own industrial and economic planning. It is important, therefore, that the student should be aware of the processes involved in economic forecasting of a short-term nature. In addition to the Treasury, which nowadays produces broad estimates for the gross national product and its components, a number of private and semi-official bodies[1] produce detailed forecasts for a year or so ahead. What follows is a general theoretical approach to economic forecasting of the gross national product and its components.

Short-term economic forecasting
The basic table used for this purpose by all the bodies concerned with forecasting the gross national product is the one on expenditure, Table 6.1., and the starting point is the quarterly series at constant (1963) prices, seasonally adjusted. Reference to this table will remind the reader that it is concerned with consumers' expenditure, public authorities' current expenditure on goods and services, gross fixed capital formation, stock change, exports and imports and the adjustment required to transform gross domestic product at market prices to factor cost. The algebraic sum of these components gives gross domestic product at factor cost, and the forecasting process requires that forecasts be made for each of these components using certain standard sources of information, together with less official material. The skill and judgement of the forecaster is also much in evidence throughout the process.

Consumers' expenditure
As we saw in Chapter 4, this is by far the largest component of total expenditure. At constant 1963 market prices it is estimated at £5,566 million, £5,661 million, £5,681 million, and £5,712 million, for the four quarters of 1969, respectively. The recognized method of estimating future consumers' expenditure is to estimate personal income, deduct from it tax and national insurance liabilities leaving 'total personal disposable income'. This, less personal saving, gives consumers' expenditure.

---

[1] Prominent among these is the National Institute of Economic and Social Research.

About 80 per cent of total personal income, as we saw in Chapter 8, comes from employment by way of wages and salaries. If one wishes to extrapolate the 1969 quarterly figures throughout 1970, attention must certainly be paid to the rapid rise in the wage index which began in the third quarter of 1969 and was continuing unabated in the first few months of 1970. The extrapolation of gross trading profits of companies is assisted by returns made to the Inland Revenue by a sample of industrial and commercial concerns. The progress of the public corporations and the like is usually indicated by these corporations in advance of their annual reports. Income from rent and self-employment can be expected to show a fairly steady rate of growth.

At this point, it is necessary to interpose the warning that short-term forecasting is undertaken on the assumption of 'unchanged policies' on the part of the government. This is of particular importance in the estimation of tax and national insurance contributions. These are related to earnings and the number of persons insured – in 1970 the upward movement from one income tax rate to a higher one may well be quite pronounced. Any changes in the tax structure operating after the April Budget cannot be taken into consideration, unless they have been announced well in advance. The deduction of tax and national insurance liabilities from personal income gives 'total personal disposable income'. This can be supplemented by personal borrowings from banks and by way of hire purchase agreements, offset, of course, by repayments.

So far the estimation has been carried on at current prices; total personal disposable income must be converted into spending at current prices and then into consumers' expenditure at constant 1963 prices. This, in turn, involves an estimation of the movements in the consumer price index during 1970. Usually personal saving is regarded as a residual, but various formulae exist to estimate it independently. All these calculations are made on a quarterly basis.

Public authorities' current expenditure on goods and services

By early 1970, most government departments had presented their estimates to Parliament and the total of these, compared with 1969 spending for the same items, gives an indication of the change at current prices.[1] This must be converted to a constant price basis. The

---

[1] A longer-term detailed forecast of public expenditure is now prepared annually.

arrangement of annual figures into quarters may present some difficulties.

Gross fixed capital formation

In the private sector this consists mainly of housing and industrial capital formation. A good indication of the number of houses likely to be completed in any one quarter can be obtained from the number of 'starts' (i.e. houses begun) a year earlier, together with the average time taken from start to finish. A large sample of firms make returns to the Ministry of Technology and the Board of Trade[1] of their expenditure on investment quarter by quarter: once in the year they are asked to estimate their investment over the next calendar year. These returns are of great value in forecasting industrial investment in the private sector. However, the figures must be corrected for biasses shown by past experience to exist, and then put on a constant price basis.

The public corporations' and public authorities' capital investment programmes are submitted to Parliament or to the responsible Minister considerably in advance; these programmes provide the basis of public investment forecasting. Again, the number of housing 'starts' in the public sector provides a means of estimating the number of houses likely to be completed.

Stocks and work in progress

Recent past figures of these are provided in returns made to the Board of Trade by a large sample of enterprises. Subsequent extrapolation must be conducted with care in the light of the so-called 'stockbuilding cycle' since it is necessary to identify the position reached in the cycle.

Exports and imports

The extrapolation of recent trends is assisted by estimates of likely growth in world output and world trade. World trade over the past few years has grown faster than world output but Britain's share of exports has decreased and her share of imports has increased. Changes in world currency reserves, devaluations or revaluations of important currencies, are further factors influencing exports and imports.

---

[1] Now combined as the Department of Trade and Industry.

Adjustment required to transform gross domestic product at market prices to factor cost

This requires a knowledge and judgement of changes in the subsidies to be paid and the incidence of indirect taxation on consumers' expenditure. Thus, in 1970, agricultural subsidies will be higher than in 1969,[1] whilst indirect taxation can, by and large, be assumed to be levied at the end-1969 rates.

Estimates of gross domestic product

The aggregation of these components, paying regard to the algebraic sign attached to each component, will give the gross domestic product at constant 1963 prices and a forecast rate of growth can thereby be calculated. In the May 1970 *Economic Review*, issued by the National Institute of Economic and Social Research, the gross domestic product in index form, for 1969 and forecasts for the next few quarters are shown thus:

Actual and forecast growth in gross domestic product

			1969	*GDP*=100
1969	I	99·1	1970 III est.	103·1
	II	99·5	IV est.	103·6
	III	100·1	1970 year est.	102·8
	IV est.	101·5	1971 I	103·8
1970	I est.	101·9	II	104·2
	II est.	102·5		

Thus, the gross domestic product in 1970 is expected to be 2·8 per cent above that for 1969.

The forecasts made under expenditure headings may be used for purposes other than that of arriving at changes in the gross national, or domestic, product as a whole. Thus, the forecasts for imports and exports assist in the estimation of the balance of payments; the prospective growth in gross domestic product can give an indication of the likely trend in unemployment during the period covered by the forecast.

Whilst this assessment of gross domestic product is from the expenditure side it is equally applicable to the demand side, expenditure

---

[1] This was known well in advance of the Budget.

being the conversion of demand into an economic reality. By increasing demand and expenditure, output is increased. This, as the late Lord Keynes and his followers showed, is a way out of economic depression and a method of increasing living standards. But is there any limit to this process? If demand is stimulated it will increase incomes and spending and, as we shall see in the next section, the movement will snowball through the multiplier effect. This can go on so long as there are unused resources of labour and capital, i.e., unemployment and spare industrial capacity. Once these unused resources are tapped, production and output cannot increase, and any further increase in demand will lead to inflation. Prices will rise, bottlenecks will develop in industry, and demand will be switched from home production to imports. At the same time, some export production will be diverted to home demand and higher costs and prices at home will make our exports less competitive. In countries such as Britain which depend greatly on their foreign trade, this increase in imports and slackening in exports will lead to balance of payments crises. The situation has recurred many times since the end of the war and measures, including devaluation of the currency, have had to be taken to check the growth in demand, particularly the demand for imports.

Of course, industrial capacity, that is, the productive potential of the industry, is not a static quantity. Industrial investment is carried out in order to increase capacity. Experts consider that over the past decade or so, industrial and commercial capacity has grown by an average of approximately 3·5 per cent a year. When all resources have been fully utilized, unemployment has dropped to about 300,000. At the time of writing (early 1970) the figure for unemployment is more than double this level because demand has been held back for a number of years now. When there is a wide margin of spare capacity, one expects relatively high unemployment; and a relationship between forecast growth in gross domestic product and the level of unemployment can be worked out. The forecast rise of 2·8 per cent in gross domestic product for 1970, referred to a little earlier, is below the expected rise in productive capacity. Hence, the forecasters expect a rise in unemployment during 1970 – on policies existing when the forecast was made.[1]

---

[1] For a much more sophisticated approach to the subject of short-term forecasting, see 'New Contributions to Economic Statistics', Fifth series, HMSO.

The use of short-term forecasting in economic management

The brief introduction to the demand/growth relationship discussed in the foregoing paragraph is but a part of the wider aspect of economic management. If demand is stimulated, expenditure grows and production rises to meet this higher demand and expenditure. Higher production means higher incomes and a fall in unemployment. The higher incomes mean more expenditure, and industry stimulated by higher demand undertakes more capital investment. This will lead ultimately to greater industrial capacity but for the time being higher capital expenditure merely adds to total demand and total output. The two major restraints on this upwards spiral are available capacity and balance of payments problems. Clearly then, the aim of the Chancellor of the Exchequer should be to contain demand within capacity and balance of payments restraints, and to take all possible steps to increase capacity by encouraging investment, research and development and greater effort on the part of workers and management. These latter are, however, rather long-term measures. Demand management is more a short-term matter.

Faced with the forecast of a rise in gross domestic product during 1970 of some 2·75 per cent, what should the Chancellor do? He and his advisers may well ask themselves three questions. Is the forecast likely to prove correct? Is the forecast rise in gross domestic product economically acceptable? (In an election year, the political implications may also be important.) Is the rise in gross domestic product coming from the right sectors and in the right amounts?

The outstanding economic events in the first half of 1970 have been the continued recovery in the balance of payments and the huge wage and salary increases demanded and, in many cases, conceded. These increases will, in the not too distant future, cause prices to rise substantially because output is not increasing at any faster rate than in 1969. Higher earnings will bring about greater real consumption until prices catch up on wages and salaries. The very much better balance of payments situation may encourage the Chancellor to turn a blind eye on these trends. Therefore, the forecast of a 2·75 per cent growth may well prove too low, especially as savings seem to be falling rather than rising.

However, if the Chancellor were to decide to limit the spending power of the public he could budget for a large surplus which, as we have seen, is a form of forced savings. This move could be assisted by limiting the growth of the money supply – a new feature in modern economic management. If the Chancellor decided to encourage investment he could reduce corporation tax and thereby leave firms more funds to use for investment. Whilst this would make economic sense, it would be electorally unpopular. If the decision is to assist consumer spending, the Chancellor has a number of choices. He can ease the squeeze on lending, reduce the level of direct taxation by raising the minimum income for taxation, reduce the standard rate of income tax or lower indirect taxation by cutting purchase tax.

Nothing has yet been said about public authorities' current expenditure on goods and services. Increased salaries in the public sector will automatically increase this at current prices. A decision to increase the real level of public authorities' current expenditure would not be popular since it would mean abandoning a recently accepted principle – that of stabilizing such expenditure. In some overseas countries, trade booms have often been export led – this means that the higher demand, leading to greater expenditure, has come from exports which have become relatively more competitive. Some of the greater demand in Britain during 1970 is expected to come from this source but the higher costs now being engendered are likely to set limits to this form of increased demand even though it is a very desirable form, economically speaking.

We end this chapter by stating the sector increases in gross domestic product expected by the National Institute of Economic and Social Research for 1970 – under pre-budget policies. The student may find it of interest, when the full results for 1970 are available, to see how far these forecasts have proved correct. The line taken by the Chancellor

Table 11.1. Short-term forecast of gross domestic product and its components*

	Percentage increase in 1970 over 1969	Proportion of total final expenditure
Gross domestic product	2·8	
Consumers' expenditure	1·7	52 per cent
Public authorities' current expenditure	3·4	13½ per cent
Gross fixed investment	4·2	15½ per cent
Exports of goods and services	5·5	19 per cent
Total final expenditure	3·0	
Stockbuilding	no change	
Imports of goods and services	3·9	

* NIESR, *Economic Review*, February 1970 (i.e. prior to the 1970 General election).

of the Exchequer and the reasons given for it will have become clear by the middle of 1970. The student should try to relate the budget proposals to the general principles of economic management enunciated in the previous paragraphs. In doing this, he should bear in mind that the NIESR suggested that demand should be stimulated to the extent of £650 million. Incidentally, a more socially acceptable phrase for stimulating demand in this way is 'reflation'.

CHAPTER 12
SUMMARY COMPARISONS OF ECONOMIC GROWTH AND FACTORS AFFECTING GROWTH IN U.K. AND OTHER OECD COUNTRIES

Introductory

Our study of the 1969 Blue Book tables will have shown that Britain has a very well developed system of national accounting. This study has concentrated only on the summary or main tables, and although the national accounts of most other OECD countries do not appear (with a few exceptions) to be as comprehensive as ours, the summary tables are available for all OECD countries. The monthly Bulletin of Statistics produced by the UN Statistical Office gives totals for gross national product or gross domestic product for a very large number of countries, together with an analysis by expenditure headings for the most recent years. The UN Statistical Yearbook gives figures for a longer run of years. Special analyses – *National Account Statistics* – give summary analyses of the kind discussed earlier in this book for the large number of UN countries spread over the world. The Organization for European Cooperation and Development (OECD) provides similar and usually more up-to-date figures and analyses for the countries now belonging to this organization. In this chapter we shall compare growth of income and output per head in O.E.C.D. countries for the period 1958–68 and glance at the way in which demand and expenditure factors constitute the gross national product, and compare the industrial sources of gross domestic product. It may be that these comparisons will throw some light on the reasons for the differing economic performances of OECD counties. Finally, we shall attempt to make some broad comparisons between the gross national product per head in OECD and Eastern Bloc countries. For the OECD study, the main source book will be *National Accounts of OECD Countries* 1957–68, supplemented by later information from the Statistical Bulletin of the United Nations.

Rates of growth in the gross domestic product in OECD countries
For this study, we are taking the period 1950–68. The year 1950
is one of the earliest for which reliable national income figures exist
in a number of OECD countries. It also marks the beginning of
the post-war economic recovery for most of the countries listed in
Table 12.1.

**Table 12.1. Average annual rates of growth in gross domestic
product 1950–68**

Country	Rate of growth per head 1950–68	1969	Country	Rate of growth per head 1950–68	1969
Canada	2·0	4·5	Italy	5·2	5·0
United States	2·2	1·8	Netherlands	3·9	5·3
Japan	7·9	12·0	Norway	3·7	4·0
Austria	4·7	5·3	Spain	(5·0)	6·5
Belgium	2·9	6·0	Sweden	3·4	4·5
Denmark	3·4	7·0	Switzerland	3·0	4·8
France	4·3	8·0	United Kingdom	2·4	2·0
Germany	4·9	7·0			

* Preliminary estimate.

There are about 20 countries in OECD as full or associated
members. In addition to those in table 12.1. Finland, Ireland, Por-
tugal and Turkey are members of the Organization. Only three are
non-European countries. The rates represent growth per head of the
employed population. In a number of cases, USA, Canada, and Germany in particular, the rate of growth in gross domestic product has
been significantly higher than gross domestic product per head. Since
1960, the growth in gross domestic product in USA has been assisted
by the absorption of millions of unemployed into active employment,
Canada has received a comparatively large influx of immigrants, and
Germany has received refugees from Eastern Germany (until 1961)
and immigrants from Italy in more recent years.

Amongst the fastest growing countries are Japan, Italy, Germany,
and possibly Spain; Austria, France, Netherlands, Norway, Denmark, and Sweden are countries of fairly average growth, with
growth in Canada, USA, Belgium, Britain and Switzerland lower
than average. Most of the countries shown in table 12.1. have had
years of little or no growth, when, on account of balance of payments
difficulties or inflationary pressure in the economy, steps have been

95

taken to restrict output. In this respect, however, the United Kingdom has the worst record. If growth in total gross national product is measured, we find that over the decade 1958 to 1968, Japan leads with an average of 10 per cent a year; Italy, Netherlands, Spain and France had growth rates of between 5.5 and 5 per cent; Germany, Denmark, Canada, USA, Switzerland, between 5 and 4·5 per cent, whilst Belgium, Sweden, and Norway had rates between 4·5 and 4 per cent. Britain was in the last place with an average of 3·3 per cent.

It is of interest to note that if gross domestic product per head grows at a rate of 3·5 per cent a year it will double itself in 20 years; at 5 per cent the doubling period is reduced to 14 years, and at 2·5 per cent it becomes 28 years. (See Appendix III.)

Gross national product per head, 1958 and 1968
Rates of growth in gross domestic product or gross national product give information on the rate at which living standards are increasing. If we want to know something of relative living standards in OECD countries, we must convert gross national product per head in the

Table 12.2. Gross National Product Per Head, 1958 and 1968

Country	$, at current rates of exchange 1958	1968
Canada	1,980	3,020
USA	2,600	4,330
Japan	340	1,410
Austria	750	1,550
Belgium	1,160	2,170
Denmark	1,400	2,550*
France	1,300	2,530
Germany	1,080	2,280
Italy	600	1,420
Netherlands	850	1,990
Norway	1,140	2,360
Spain	300	780*
Sweden	1,510	3,230
Switzerland	1,410	2,770
United Kingdom	1,250	1,850*

Source: 'National Accounts of OECD Countries'

* Currency devaluation, November 1967, Spain and UK by 14 per cent; Denmark by 7 per cent,

currency of each country into that of a common currency – usually US dollars. This has to be done at the rate of exchange ruling at the time. It is by no means an ideal method but it is the best one available. It implies that the rate of exchange accurately equates the purchasing power of the countries in question, and it involves a sudden reduction in gross national product per head in the case of currency devaluation. Britain, Spain, and Denmark devalued their currencies in November 1967 and this move has reduced their gross national product per head figures expressed in dollars.

By 1968, Britain had fallen to the eleventh place in the 15 OECD countries for which figures are quoted above (a drop of five places in ten years). At present rates of growth, Japan will have overtaken Britain by the end of 1972. The devaluation of the French franc and the upwards revaluation of the German mark in 1969 have brought the two countries into approximate equality so far as gross national product per head is concerned.

As we have pointed out earlier, comparative living standards depend upon consumers' expenditure per head and the volume of goods which can be bought with this expenditure. Consumers' expenditure in Britain tends to be a higher proportion of gross national product than in other OECD countries whilst prices of consumer goods tend to be lower. Hence, current living standards in Britain are rather higher than the figure of $1,850 per head would suggest. Appendix V compares consumer price index numbers in various OECD capitals.

Expenditure on gross national product in OECD countries.
Table 12.3. gives, in percentage terms, the share of gross national product generated by the three main components – consumers' expenditure, public authorities' current expenditure and gross domestic fixed capital formation. These percentages do not amount to exactly 100 per cent since stockbuilding, net exports, and property income from abroad are omitted. Any of these three factors could be negative but in total they represent only a small part of gross national product.

Perhaps the main interest in this table lies in the proportion of gross national product devoted to, and derived from, investment. This varies from 16·8 per cent in the case of USA and 18 per cent in Britain to 28·8 per cent in Norway and 39·9 per cent in Japan. Generally speaking, the higher the proportion of national output derived from consumer spending, the lower is that from investment. The latter

Table 12.3. Proportion of gross national product generated by main components

Country	Consumers' expenditure	PA current expenditure	Gross fixed capital formation
	Average 1966–68 as percentage		
Canada	60·6	15·1	24·6
USA	61·5	20·5	16·8
Japan	53·3	8·6	39·9
Austria	59·3	14·6	24·9
Belgium	64·5	13·5	21·0
Denmark	63·0	16·9	21·0
France	60·2	12·4	24·9
West Germany	57·0	16·0	23·6
Italy	64·2	13·5	18·9
Netherlands	57·0	15·6	26·1
Norway	54·1	17·3	28·8
Spain	69·6	9·9	21·6
Sweden	55·5	21·1	23·9
Switzerland	58·6	11·7	25·5
United Kingdom	63·6	17·6	18·0

Source: United Nations Monthly Bulletin of Statistics.

can only come from savings of one kind or another. Public authorities' current expenditure is the third most important generating force in output except in the case of USA and Britain. This expenditure may reflect, to a certain extent, the level of defence and similar expenditure (space research, etc.) as in USA and Britain, but it more often is a reflection of social attitudes. The Scandinavian countries have a long socialist tradition and the welfare state concept is deeply entrenched. As a consequence, public authorities' current expenditure is higher than average. Japan has a negligible defence expenditure and comparatively backward social services, hence public expenditure is low: this also applies to Spain. In the case of Switzerland, a comparatively wealthy country, the low public expenditure is occasioned by an individualistic, as opposed to socialistic, attitude of mind.

The thought must have occurred to readers that economic growth is fairly closely associated with the level of investment. If one compares tables 12.1. and 12.3. there is evidence that the higher the proportion of gross national product devoted to investment, the greater the rate of growth seems to be. Readers with an elementary knowledge of statistics will be able to work out the coefficient of correlation. (The rank coefficient works out at 0·33.[1]) However, as pointed out in the discussions on investment in Britain, it is investment in factories and plant and machinery which is most likely to affect growth; social investment (houses, schools, hospitals) may have no large direct effect on national output. It is of interest, therefore, to consider what proportion of total investment can be regarded as industrial, as opposed to social.

The best that can be done in this respect for OECD countries taken as a whole is to take from the total capital formation, investment in residential buildings. This will still leave schools and hospitals in the remainder but as the investment in these is not stated there is no other course open. In 1967 the remainder varied from 68·0 per cent of total investment in Italy to 85·8 per cent in Norway, with an OECD average of 78·2 per cent. Countries whose industrial investment accounted for a higher proportion of total investment than this were Canada, USA, Japan, Austria, Norway, Spain, and Britain. Denmark was exactly average. In general, the countries with the highest proportion of investment to gross national product are those with the highest proportion of industrial investment to total investment. Britain, along with the USA, is a conspicuous exception. Little, therefore, would be gained by associating growth rates with industrial investment as defined above.

Industrial derivation of gross national product

In Chapter 4 we considered the industrial and services source of gross national product in Britain. We saw what proportion of total national output was derived from agriculture, mining, manufacturing industries, construction, etc., and from a range of service industries such as distribution, transport, public health services and so on. Most other OECD countries produce figures showing the industrial and service origin of gross national product, and these estimates provide a good deal of useful information about the economies of the countries concerned. They are tabulated as percentages (for 1967) for the 15 countries distinguished in the analyses which have already been made in the present chapter (Table 12.4.).

---

[1] Not a very marked association.

Table 12.4. Gross domestic product at factor cost by industry of origin (1967)
Percentages

	1	2	3	4	5	6	7	8	9	10	11	12
Canada	5·9	4·1	25·1	6·1	3·2	8·6	13·6	6·8	3·3	7·3	15·8	
United States*	3·1	1·8	28·1	4·5	2·4	6·3	16·2	6·2	7·4	13·7	10·7	
Japan	11·6	0·8	28·5	7·3		8·9	16·9		9·4		4·2	12·2
Austria	8·6		36·8	11·8	3·1	7·1	8·3	4·0	0·9	12·2	2·3	4·9
Belgium	5·6	1·9	29·7	7·2	2·1	7·5	10·6	4·1	6·3	7·1	7·1	10·7
Denmark^a	10·6	0·06	32·3	10·8	2·0	11·2	15·8	3·4	6·1	15·6		5·2
France^b	7·4	1·3	35·2	9·0	1·8	4·9	13·7	0·8^d	4·1	9·0	4·3	8·6
West Germany	4·1	3·8	39·0	6·8	1·9	5·9	13·7	3·8	4·2	9·6		9·0
Italy	12·4	0·8	28·7	8·3	2·7	7·0	9·9	4·9	5·0	12·2		8·2
Netherlands	7·2	1·2	32·0	6·8	2·2	8·4	12·3	2·9	2·9	8·8		15·5
Norway	7·5	1·1	25·9	8·4	2·9	18·1	12·8	2·5	3·0	4·9	7·2	5·8
Spain	16·4	1·1	26·4	5·2	2·0	6·3	12·5	4·5	3·5	6·7	3·0	12·4
Sweden*	5·0	0·8	27·9	9·3	2·5	7·1	20·6	4·0	4·6	4·6	9·5	4·4
Switzerland^c	6·4	–	36·8	9·8	3·0	7·0	16·5		–	20·5		–
United Kingdom	3·3	2·1	33·6	7·1	3·3	8·3	11·1	2·3	4·8	7·1	5·0	12·8

Source: National Accounts of OECD Countries.

* Analysis is at market prices.

^a Large negative adjustments to total cannot be allocated.

^b 1966 figures.

^c Source OECD Economic Survey, January 1970.
  Excludes foreign earnings.

The headings in this table have been numbered in order to save space and the numbers in question represent the following categories:

1. Agriculture, forestry and fishing
2. Mining
3. Manufacturing
4. Construction
5. Electricity, gas and water
6. Transportation and communication
7. Wholesale and retail trade
8. Banking, insurance, etc.
9. Ownership of buildings
10. Public administration and defence
11. Health and educational services
12. Miscellaneous services

We repeat that these percentages are worth studying for the light which they throw on the economies of the various countries. A fairly wide variation exists in the proportion of gross national product derived from agriculture. In terms of output per man, this sector is perhaps the least efficient in each of the countries taken separately. Moreover, it is the reservoir from which manpower may be drawn to build up the labour force in factories and cities. Hence it is the aim of most countries to mechanize their agriculture, persuade the small and inefficient farmers to leave the land, and use the manpower so set free in more profitable sectors. Japan, Italy and Spain appear to have large reserves of manpower in agriculture in its various forms. For this reason alone one would expect that economic growth in these countries would continue to be stimulated by transfers of labour from inefficient to more efficient industries. This process is always part of the industrial take-off stage.

Mining, nowadays, in OECD countries at least, is of little more than marginal importance in the various countries' economies. Manufacturing industry provides about 30 to 33 per cent of gross national product on an average. It is of relatively less importance where agriculture is of more than average importance and in the affluent societies such as Sweden and the USA where the service industries and occupations account for such a large proportion of gross national product. It may come as a surprise to see that Denmark, Austria and Switzerland derive such a comparatively large proportion of total national income from manufacturing. Germany is the most highly industrialized country in OECD with France, Switzerland, Britain and the Netherlands not far behind.

Construction and the electricity, gas, and water industries, together produce about 9 per cent of the output in OECD countries taken as a whole and there is comparatively little deviation from this average on the part of individual countries. Transportation and communication produce about as much as construction, with the one glaring exception of Norway, which relies very heavily on its merchant fleet for its very high return from transportation. It is difficult to find any consistent pattern in the share of gross national product emanating from wholesale and retail distribution. On the whole, the share of gross national product obtained from this source increases with the growth in affluence, and the three leaders in the affluence stakes, USA, Canada and Sweden head the list, with Denmark, France and West Germany following. But Japan and Spain rely more heavily on distribution than does Belgium and the United Kingdom. Banking,

101

insurance and real estate business are relatively most important in USA and Canada, where real estate business is still quite significant. Otherwise, the average is around 4 per cent, with France exceptionally low for the reason given in the footnote. Ownership of buildings produces much the same proportion as does banking, insurance, etc.

The remaining three headings cover income derived from public administration; viz defence and welfare services and miscellaneous services of a personal nature. Lack of information makes it difficult to comment upon these figures. Column 10 represents defence and general administration, Column 11, the social and welfare services – or at least the incomes they provide – and 12 is miscellaneous services. Column 10 is high in the USA on account of its defence and research effort and high in Italy because of its very large public service which runs, amongst other services, its main transport systems. The Scandinavian countries have well-developed State welfare and education services. Miscellaneous services rank high in Spain, possibly because personal service to families, now non-existent in Britain and many other countries, is still very common. The high figure for Britain may well be at the expense of distribution; hairdressing, for example, may be regarded by some countries as forming part of the retail trade; in Britain it is regarded as a service industry.

Relative output in OECD countries

It would be unwise to conclude this study of the economies of OECD countries as revealed by their national income accounts without providing some information on the relative size of the gross national product of these countries. Table 12.5. shows this in two ways. First, the 1968 estimate of gross national product with which the gross national product per head figures in table 12.2. are related: these are expressed in dollars at current 1968 prices. Second, the 1963 gross national product expressed in dollars are extrapolated to 1969 in accordance with growth rates applicable to each country. The resulting figures are then expressed as a percentage of total gross national product in OECD countries. These figures therefore represent the contribution, at constant 1963 prices, of each country to 1969 total OECD output at constant 1963 prices. This eliminates the effect of differing rates of price increases in the various countries since 1963.

From the table it will be seen that USA has rather less than one-third of the total population of the 15 OECD countries but more than half the total gross national product. At current 1968 prices, Japan ranked second to USA, just beating West Germany. At constant

Table 12.5. Total and relative output in OECD countries

Country	GNP per head 1968 $	Population 1968 (millions)	GNP 1968 $ billions[c]	Percentage of GNP (1969) of OECD countries
Canada	3,020	20·772	62·731	3·6
United States	4,330	201·152	870·988	52·8
Japan	1,410	101·080	142·523	8·3
Austria	1,550	7·350	11·393	0·7
Belgium	2,170	9·619	20·873	1·3
Denmark	2,550[a]	4·870	12·419	0·7
France	2,530	49·920	126·298	7·4
West Germany	2,280	58·015[b]	132·274	8·5
Italy	1,420	52·750	94·905	4·3
Netherlands	1,990	12·743	25·359	1·3
Norway	2,360	3·819	9·013	0·5
Spain	780[a]	32·621	25·444	1·4
Sweden	3,230	7·918	25·575	1·4
Switzerland	2,770	6·147	17·027	1·0
United Kingdom	1,850[a]	55·283	102·274	6·8
Total (Average)	2,660	624·059	1,659·06	100·0

[a] Currency devaluation, November 1967.

[b] Includes West Berlin.

[c] 1,000 million.

Note: The method used in obtaining the percentages in column 5 ignores the currency devaluations and revaluation which took place in 1967 and 1969.

prices, however, Germany was just ahead in 1969 (apart from any revaluation effect). It is of interest to compare the European Economic Community with USA. The total population of the six (Luxemburg is very small but an allowance has been made in the totals) in 1968 was 183·5 million, and their combined gross national product was $380 billion. Thus, the six have a population equal to 90 per cent, and a combined gross national product of 44 per cent, of those for USA.

Factors affecting growth in industrial countries

We have already seen that the rate of economic growth can depend upon the degree of industrialization already achieved. The rate tends to be greater than average as manufacturing industry grows in importance. Spectacular increases in output can be achieved from the large-scale introduction of industrialization into countries which were formerly mainly agricultural – for example, Japan, Italy and, more recently, Spain. Generally speaking, the higher the proportion of gross national product derived from manufacturing industry, the higher the growth rate will tend to be. But as affluence grows, the inhabitants of any country tend to demand more and better services, and manufacturing industry may decline in importance relative to services, as in the United States and Sweden. In Germany, where affluence is of more recent origin, the importance of manufacturing industry, and therefore the rate of growth, is being sustained by a thrusting and efficient export policy. In Britain, the relative lack of such a policy has resulted in repeated balance of payments crises and the deliberate restraining of economic growth in order to overcome them.

In countries which have achieved about the same degree of industrialization, it certainly seems that a high rate of industrial and social investment goes hand in hand with a high rate of economic growth, but too much importance should not be attached to this connection. The whole question of isolating the factors affecting economic growth is one of great difficulty and these factors may be psychological as well as economic. By the first is meant the national approach to growth. The fact that the British people are reluctant or unwilling to link higher earnings with higher productivity, and set such great store by immediate consumption rather than savings, means that they are choosing inflation, restrictive practices, and slow economic growth in preference to effort, restraint in spending and average or high growth. Amongst the economic factors, which are generally considered to have an important effect on growth but the effect of which it is extremely difficult to measure, are the quality of management and the extent and quality of the education and training received by the average citizen.

In a book written a few years ago, *Britain's Economic Prospects*, a team of American and Canadian economists analysed the performance of the British economy and the effectiveness of Britain's economic policies. The authors make a great deal of the poor quality of British management compared with that obtaining in the United States of America. This poor quality manifests itself in the relatively low output per worker in Britain; the average worker in USA produces three times as much as his British counterpart. This comes about mainly on account of overmanning and restrictive practices. It is easy to say that management in Britain ought to sweep away these restrictive practices and drastically reduce this overmanning, but the entire political and social atmosphere is against this. Redundancy is unpopular in both trade union and political circles, and attempts to introduce what are often called 'American' methods into British industry are usually firmly resisted. Recent happenings in the docks, ship-yards, and the printing industry show how strong is the feeling against the removal of restrictive practices and the reduction of overmanning. These practices exist as much in the public as the private sector. Moreover, in the past, the public services have often been the pace-setters in each round of wage increases.

Nearly a decade ago, Professor Edward Denison of the Brookings Institution,[1] and a contributor to *Britain's Economic Prospects*, analysed the sources of economic growth in USA over the period 1929–57. The average increase in output per head over the 30-year span was 1·6 per cent, per annum. A regression analysis ascribed rather less than 10 per cent of the whole to increased capital per head, 40 per cent was deemed to have come from improved education and training, 17 per cent from economies of scale due to the expansion of demand over the period covered, and about 35 per cent from the results of research developments and innovation. There was a small negative contribution arising from shorter working hours and longer holidays. It would not be entirely reasonable to apply US findings to British conditions; but it is of interest to note that in the proportion of gross national product devoted to education and research and development, Britain compares very favourably with European industrial countries and fairly favourably with USA. Which points to the conclusion that the type of education and training, and research development and innovation which are current in Britain are not orientated towards economic growth.

Economic growth in USSR and the eastern bloc

In assessing gross national product in these countries and comparing it with that of OECD countries, two rather intractable problems emerge. In the first place, the 'socialist' republics do not define gross national product in the same way as the West. As Marxist countries, they make a distinction between 'productive' and 'unproductive' labour. Payment for the latter is regarded as transfer incomes. This rules out the incomes of public servants and other important groups

---

[1] Washington D.C., U.S.A.

105

of workers. (And there are no rentiers in Marxist economics.) The result of aggregating incomes on this basis is called 'net material product' which, by definition, is significantly less than gross national product. Secondly, the Eastern bloc countries form a fairly closed economic group; they trade extensively with one another but very little with the outside world. Hence the nominal rates of exchange which they quote may have little reference to relative purchasing power. Those bloc countries which really encourage tourists and foreign trade quote non-commercial rates which may differ enormously from basic rates. For example, in Bulgaria 1·17 and 2·00 levs to $1; in Romania 6·0 and 12·0 – 18·0 leu to $1. Thus, even if we knew the gross national product equivalents in national currencies we could not convert them to dollars merely by using exchange rates.

However, a number of experts have turned their attention to comparing national output in the USSR and other bloc countries with that in the USA in a number of ways. There are two basic methods employed; estimating the difference between gross national product and net material product, and estimating gross national product directly by using whatever output figures are available in physical (i.e. non-monetary) terms and comparing these with US output in physical and monetary terms. USSR and US outputs of many important products are known. These are valued in US prices and the comparison gives gross national product in USSR at US prices. The estimation of gross national product from individual incomes gives a figure in roubles – i.e. USSR currency. From these two results a purchasing power parity can be worked out between dollars and roubles.

Estimates appearing in *Economic Growth in Japan and the USSR* by Angus Maddison suggest that in 1965 the gross national product of USSR at US prices was 60 per cent of that of USA and that the official dollar-rouble rate of 0·9 roubles to the dollar overvalued the latter by nearly one-tenth. In 1965, the population of USA was 194·6 million and that USSR 230·56 million: *per capita*, the 1965 output in USSR was therefore about half that of USA. Since 1965, the ratio could have moved fractionally in favour of USSR. Compared with Britain, gross national product per head in USSR would be about the same or perhaps a little lower. Consumption per head is a better measure of relative living standards and since government expenditure and capital investment loom very large in the USSR economy, the figures of real consumption per head in 1965 are much less favourable to the latter country. Maddison suggests that in UK the figure was 70 per cent, and in USSR 40 per cent, of the US level. Again, it has to be remembered that in Russia the social services are all provided by the State at no direct cost to the individual; allowance for this would significantly improve the USSR rate.

One important feature of the economy of the USSR is the vast number of persons employed in agriculture, some 30 per cent of the total in employment in 1965, or about five times the US level, and eight times that of UK. Agricultural output per head is certainly much lower than industrial output per head in Russia.

The Monthly Bulletin of Statistics of the United Nations[1] gives estimates of net material product for all Eastern bloc countries and analyses it into individual (personal) consumption, government consumption, investment, etc. From these figures it is possible to compare net material product per head with that of the USSR, and hence with that of the USA. (Figures of net material product at constant prices are also given.) The same volume gives index numbers of industrial production in all the Eastern bloc countries. Rates of growth in both net material product and in industrial production in these countries are generally significantly higher than in OECD countries (except Japan). Thus, in the eight years from 1960–68, industrial production rose by about 60 per cent in OECD countries but by about 95 per cent in Eastern Europe. Growth in agricultural output still lags behind OECD standards.

---

[1] Similar information for longer periods is given in *UN Statistical Year Books*.

APPENDICES

Appendix I (a) The growth of national income, 1855–1959

	Net national income at factor cost in current prices	National income per head current prices	National income per head at 1913–14 prices
	£ million	£	£
1855	627	22·54	19·77
1865	811	27·10	23·98
1875	1,085	33·04	29·77
1885	1,124	31·21	34·29
1895	1,449	36·94	44·51
1905	1,832	42·62	46·84
1914	2,294	49·77	50·27
1925	4,091	90·79	47·79
1935	4,238	90·42	55·82
1945	8,285	168·46	66·06
1955	15,416	302·46	71·67
1959	18,391	364·16	77·98

Extracts from Table 90 of *British Economic Growth 1688–1959*, Deane and Cole. Annual figures are quoted from 1855 onwards. For earlier periods, estimates are given for census years, mainly in other tables of the book.

Appendix I (b) Distribution of the occupied population of the United Kingdom, 1851–1911
(millions)

	1851	1881	1911
Agriculture, forestry, fishing	3·6	2·6	2·3
Mining and quarrying	0·4	0·7	1·2
Manufacturing	3·9	4·5	6·1
Building and construction	0·6	1·0	1·2
Trade and commerce	1·2	2·2	3·1
Transport	0·4	0·8	1·7
Domestic service	1·5	2·4	2·2
Public and professional service	0·5	0·8	1·5
All other	0·6	0·7	0·8
Total occupied	12·7	15·7	20·2

Appendix I (c) Trends in Consumers' expenditure, Capital formation etc., since 1860

Between 1860 and 1900, consumers' expenditure generated about 84 per cent of gross national product at market prices, public authorities' current expenditure about 5 per cent, gross domestic fixed capital about 7 per cent, and net foreign investment about 4 per cent. Over the period, consumers' expenditure tended to decline and gross domestic fixed capital to rise. As late as 1935, consumers' expenditure equalled 81 per cent of gross national product, public authorities' current expenditure 9·5 per cent, gross domestic fixed capital 9 per cent and net foreign investment 0·5 per cent.

Estimated from table 91 of *British Economic Growth 1688–1959*.

Appendix II (a) Economic growth in industrial countries*
Recent and long-term growth rates in national product per man-year

	Long-term rate		1950–59	1954–59
	Starting year	Rate Per cent per annum	Per cent per annum	
Japan	1,880	2·9	6·1	7·6
Italy	1,863	1·2	4·7	3·8
Germany	1.853	1·5	4·5	3·6
France	1,855	1·5	3·6	3·3
Netherlands	1,900	1·1	3·4	2·9
Norway	1,865	1·6	3·1	2·5
Sweden	1,863	2·1	2·8	3·0
United States	1,871	2·0	2·2	2·2
Canada	1,872	1·7	2·0	1·8
Denmark	1,872	1·6	1·8	2·5
United Kingdom	1,857	1·2	1·7	1·6

* Table 1 in 'Economic Growth: The Last Hundred Years' *Economic Review* no. 16, *NIESR*.

Appendix II (b) The level of real product per head in ten countries in relation to that of the United Kingdom 1871/75 to 1959

	1871/5	1900/4	1909/13	1922	1938	1950	1959
United Kingdom	100	100	100	100	100	100	100
United States	84	116	126	153	129	184	181
Canada	74	89	101	104	86	127	121

Appendix II (b) *continued*

	1871/5	1900/4	1909/13	1922	1938	1950	1959
France			91	94	82	83	95
Netherlands		76	77	99	80	80	92
Denmark	66	71	85	94	93	99	100
Norway	66	52	58	77	87	93	99
Sweden	61	63	76	86	97	115	124
Germany	61	68	73	72	82	65	96
Italy	54	38	42	53	48	42	55
Japan		11	12	18	24	16	26

* Table 7 in 'Economic Growth: The Last Hundred Years', *Economic Review* No. 16, *NIESR*.

Appendix III. The calculation of rates of growth

1. This is a simple algebraic problem and is identical with that of calculating the rate of interest involved in compound interest calculations.
2. Example: taking the year 1963 = 100, the index of industrial production in France, Germany and Britain was 74, 71 and 85 respectively in 1957, and 142, 144 and 123 in 1969. Calculate the average annual increase in each case.
3. The formula[1] $A = PR^n$ applies to all such growth problems. A represents the level achieved in the final year quoted, P that in the starting year. $R = 1 + \dfrac{\text{rate of growth}}{100}$, and n, the time span in years. We require the rate of growth as a percentage; this necessitates calculating R which can only be done by the use of logarithms.
4. Going back to the basic formula and taking logarithms we get:

$\log A = \log P + n \log R$, or $\log R = \dfrac{\log A - \log P}{n}$.

In the case of France,

$\log R = \dfrac{\log 142 - \log 74}{12} = \dfrac{2 \cdot 1523 - 1 \cdot 8692}{12} = \dfrac{0.2831}{12}$

Therefore $R = \text{antilog } 0.0236 = 1.055$

Therefore $1.055 = 1 + \dfrac{\text{rate of growth}}{100}$

Therefore $105 \cdot 5 = 100 + \text{rate of growth}$

Therefore rate of growth $= 5 \cdot 5$ per cent per annum.

---

[1] The graphical representation of A and n is sometimes called an 'exponential curve'.

The student may wish to satisfy himself that the average growth rates for Germany and Britain were 6·0 per cent and 3·1 per cent, respectively.

5. If the figures show a decline, R will be less than 1·000 and the rate of growth, r, a minus quantity.

6. Example: Employment in mining and quarrying in Britain was 874,000 in 1954 and 557,000 in 1967. What was the average annual rate of decline?

7. $\log R = \dfrac{\log 557 - \log 874}{13} = \dfrac{2.7459 - 2.9415}{13} = \dfrac{-.8044}{14} = 1.9850$

Antilog $R = 0.9661$ and $r = -3.4$ per cent; or, the rate of decline is 3·4 per cent per annum.

8. Finally, a quick method of estimating the time taken for any variable to double itself at a given rate of growth. Divide 70 by the rate of growth. Thus, if production grows at 5 per cent it will double itself in 14 years. Conversely, if a variable doubles itself in 10 years, the average annual rate of growth will be 7 per cent. The student may be interested to find a theoretical justification for this rule.

Appendix IV. Net output per person in manufacturing industries in 1963 and 1968

Net output per person employed — £'s sterling

	1963	1968
All Manufacturing	1,364	1,982
Food, drink and tobacco	1,697	2,485
Coal and petroleum products	2,494	4,229
Chemicals and allied industries	2,310	3,385
Metal manufacture	1,447	1,958
Mechanical engineering	1,359	2,002
Instrument engineering	1,261	1,700
Electrical engineering	1,246	1,827
Shipbuilding and marine engineering	1,082	1,587
Vehicles	1,454	2,078
Metal goods	1,225	1,764
Textiles	1,058	£,574
Leather, leather goods, fur	1,107	1,551
Clothing and footwear	768	1,102
Bricks, pottery, glass, cement	1,355	1,986
Timber, furniture, etc	1,149	1,776
Paper, printing, and publishing	1,448	2,041
Other manufacturing	1,435	2,076

111

Appendix IV *continued*

	1963	*1968*
Non-manufacturing industries		
Mining and quarrying	1,190	1,672
Construction	1,093	1,745
Gas, electricity and water	2,417	3,859

Appendix V. Retail price comparisons in various OECD countries
New York City = 100

City	OECD Country	Date		Total Index Excluding housing
Athens	Greece	June 1969	86	92
Bonn	West Germany	July 1969 [a]	87	90
Copenhagen	Denmark	July 1969	85	91
Geneva	Switzerland	August 1969	82	90
The Hague	Netherlands	September 1969	81	87
London	United Kingdom	August 1969	83	92
Montreal	Canada	August 1969	84	89
Paris	France	September 1969 [b]	91	96
Rome	Italy	March 1969	83	91
Vienna	Austria	October 1968	81	91
Washington D.C.	USA	August 1969	93	96

[a] Pre-revaluation figure
[b] Post-devaluation figure

The above figures have been taken from a Special Table which appears twice a year in the UN Monthly Bulletin of Statistics. The table is headed 'Retail price comparisons to determine salary differentials of United Nations officials'. The figures represent comparative cost-of-living figures in some 100 centres where UN officials operate. The comparison is made with New York City. The figures which relate to OECD countries have been extracted.

It will be noted that the total index for non-USA centres averages 84. This implies that at the rate of exchange prevailing at the time, the average cost of living in the OECD centres named above for middle-class professional men was about five-sixths of that in New York. To that extent, the dollar was overvalued by one-fifth – at least so far as consumers' goods and services are concerned. It will be further noted that when 'housing' is excluded, the differential is much reduced. Thus 'housing' (hotel accommodation, flats, etc.) accounts for a large part of the differential; its cost is relatively much higher in New York than in OECD (and other) countries. Prices in London were about average, at least so far as the purchases made by professional men are concerned. This may cause some surprise in view of the prevalent popular ideas on the subject.

Whilst Appendix V covers only retail prices for a specific category of goods and services, its implications should be borne in mind when considering the use of exchange rates to convert gross national product figures in various OECD countries to dollars (Chapter 12).

EXERCISES AND ESSAY QUESTIONS

(1) Using the UN Monthly Bulletin of Statistics, or a similar source, draw up a table showing gross national product per head for 1969 (or 1968) for some 25 countries divided more or less equally into subsistence economies, subsistence economies with primary and secondary industries, countries at the industrial take-off stage, moderately advanced industrial countries, and affluent societies.

(2) How has the real national income per head changed in the United Kingdom in the past 20 years? What do you consider to be the chief causes of this change?

(3) National income = national product = national expenditure. Explain this relationship and discuss its significance for the measurement of national income.

(4) Economic growth in Britain over the past 15 years has been slower than in most other industrial countries. Suggest reasons for this.

(5) Distinguish between gross national product at factor cost and at market prices, and between gross national product and national income.

(6) Explain what you understand by the term 'productivity' and discuss the factors which influence it.

(7) What do you understand by consumers' expenditure, gross domestic capital formation, and public authorities' current expenditure on goods and services.

(8) Show clearly, by using the 1970 Blue Book figures, how investment in Britain was financed in 1969.

(9) Draw up a table of available resources and their allocation for 1959 and 1969 and comment upon any significant changes which have taken place.

(10) Explain what is meant by real national product. How is it measured?

(11) 'The percentage of income spent on food declines as income increases.' What statistical evidence is there in Britain of the truth of this statement?

(12) How important is it for Britain to increase the proportion of

national income devoted to gross capital formation if she wishes to increase her rate of growth?

(13) What is meant by a Lorenz Curve? Show how it may be used to indicate the degree of inequality in incomes.

(14) Study the figures in columns (2), (3) and (4) of the following table and explain precisely what information you can derive from them:

Gross national product per head in the United Kingdom

(1)	(2)	(3)	(4)
	Gross national product per head, current prices	Price Index 1921=100	Gross national product per head, 1921 prices
Year			
	£		£
1921	116·3	100	116·3
1931	91·0	66·2	137·5
1951	256·6	135·2	189·8
1961	457·7	197·9	231·3

(15) Define: imputed income; stock appreciation; capital consumption; capital stock.

(16) Draw up a table showing the industrial sources of gross national product for 1969, for Britain, the United States, and Japan. Comment critically upon the differences brought out.

(17) Explain why a British manufacturer may be unable to compete with an American firm paying much higher wages, and also with a Japanese firm paying lower wages.

(18) Assemble what summary data you can which shows the relative level of industrial wages in Britain, the USA and Japan in 1959 and 1969.

(19) What do you understand by economic growth? Should it be the over-riding aim of government policy?

(20) What difficulties arise in trying to compare the standards of living in two different countries?

(21) Draw up a table showing gross national product by category of expenditure for 1968 in Britain, Germany, and the Netherlands. Comment upon any significant differences between the British figures and those of the other two countries.

(22) Write notes on: gross and net output; the perpetual inventory method of estimating capital stock; work in progress.

(23) Draw up a table showing receipts on current account for the central government for 1959 and 1969 and comment on the differences brought out.

(24) Explain, with reference to 1969 figures, the method of arriving at gross national product from factor incomes.

(25) Write an essay on the use of quarterly national income tables in economic forecasting.

(26) Using the 'Treasury analysis of public expenditure' tables in the 1970 Blue Book, indicate the main changes which have taken place in this expenditure between 1959 and 1969.

(27) What part has personal savings played in the finance of investment from 1950 to 1970?

(28) What do you understand by 'personal disposable income' and 'real disposable income'? Using the National Institute's *Economic Reviews* for February and May 1970 (Nos. 51 and 52), demonstrate the economic futility of the large wage increases awarded in the period July 1969–June 1970.

(29) Discuss the importance of 'sector' price index numbers in national income accounting.

(30) Draw up an appropriation account for companies for 1959 and 1969 and comment on the significant changes which have occurred over the decade.

(31) Write an account (centred around a statistical table) of the variations in net output per person employed in manufacturing industries as shown in the provisional results of the 1968 census of production.

(32) Using OECD publications on employment and national accounts, draw up a table comparing output per person employed in agriculture, manufacturing industry and construction in UK, USA, Germany, and Japan for the most recent year possible.

BIBLIOGRAPHY

(1) Publications mentioned by title (and author) in the text.

Dictionary of Economics, Seldon and Pennance, J. M. Dent
The Economics of Welfare, A. C. Pigou, Macmillan
National Income and Outlay, Colin Clarke, Macmillan
British Economic Growth 1688–1959, P. M. Deane and W. A. Cole, Cambridge University Press
National Income and Expenditure of the United Kingdom, 1870–1962, James B. Jefferys and Dorothy Walters, Reprint series, NIESR
Economic Review, NIESR (Quarterly)
National Accounts Statistics – Sources and Methods, HMSO
Blue Books, National Income and Expenditure, HMSO (Annually)
Family Expenditure Survey, HMSO (Annually)
Economic Growth in Japan and USSR, Angus Maddison, Allen and Unwin
National Food Survey, Ministry of Agriculture and Food, HMSO (Annually)
International Passenger Survey, Board of Trade, HMSO (Annually)
Monthly Digest of Statistics, HMSO (Monthly)
Economic Trends, HMSO (Quarterly)
New Contributions to Economic Statistics, Fifth Series, HMSO
Monthly Bulletin of Statistics, United Nations
Statistical Year Books, United Nations
National Accounts of OECD Countries, OECD (Annually)
Sources of Economic Growth in the USA, E. F. Denison, Brookings Institution
Britain's Economic Prospects, Richard E. Caves and associates, Allen and Unwin

(2) Publications not mentioned specifically but of obvious reference value in a study of national income and expenditure.

National Income 1924–31, Colin Clark, Macmillan
The National Income 1924, A. L. Bowley and Josiah Stamp, Colin Clark, Macmillan
A System of National Accounts and Supporting Tables, United Nations
International Comparisons of Real Income, OECD

NATIONAL INCOME AND EXPENDITURE

'Net Investment in Fixed Assets in UK 1938–53', P. Redfern, *Journal of the Royal Statistical Society*, vol. 118, part 2.

'The Stock of Fixed Capital in the UK in 1961', G. Dean, *Journal of the Royal Statistical Society*, vol. 127, part 3.

National Income and Social Accounting, Edey and Peacock, Hutchinson's University Library

'National Income of the United Kingdom 1870–1946', A. R. Prest, *Economic Journal*

Why Growth Rates Differ, E. F. Denison and J. P. Poullier, Brookings Institution

Management of the British Economy 1945–60, J. C. R. Dow, Cambridge University Press

Comparative National Products and Price Levels, OEEC

The Stages of Economic Growth, W. W. Rostow, Cambridge University Press

INDEX